SENTENCE
SERMONS

Compiled by Dean R. Zimmerman

SENTENCE SERMONS

Deseret Book Company
Salt Lake City, Utah
1978

Library of Congress Cataloging in Publication Data
Main entry under title:

Sentence sermons.

    1. Mormons and Mormonism—Quotations, maxims, etc.
I. Zimmerman, Dean R.
BX8608.5.S46   230′.9′3   78-2568
ISBN 0-87747-672-1

To my parents, S. Rex and Ardell Marie Dean Zimmerman. The integrity of their lives is an inspiration to their children and grandchildren.

CONTENTS

PREFACE

"We remember the last conference as the best conference that we ever had because we are close to it," Elder George Albert Smith of the Council of the Twelve declared at the semiannual general conference of the Church on October 6, 1934. "How fine it would be," he continued, "if we could remember all the truths that we have heard in other conferences, not only remember them now, but if we could treasure them during life—retaining the teachings of the Lord which came to us through his servants." (*Conference Report,* October 1934, pp. 51-52.)

Sentence Sermons unlocks that treasury.

Every address by the General Authorities of The Church of Jesus Christ of Latter-day Saints as published in the *History of the Church* (1820-1848), *Journal of Discourses* (1839-1886), *Conference Reports* (1880-1976) and *Area Conference Reports* (1971-1974) has been searched for brief expressions of universal or eternal truths. These statements, or sentence sermons, reflect profound insight into the human heart, mortality, eternity, governmental and world affairs, and the gospel of Jesus Christ.

Quotations in this volume have been selected for their brief, poetic (in the broadest sense of the term) expression of truth, humor, or practical wisdom. Because they are taken from speeches, they are especially suited for oral delivery. Everyone who gives talks or teaches, and all who find joy in succinct expressions of truth, will find this an uplifting and resourceful volume.

Where expressions by different speakers are substantially the same, the earliest expression has been selected. Where certain statements are repeated by a speaker, preference has usually been given to the earliest citation. Exceptions occur where the restatement is more general in its application or is better stated. Obviously, the selection is subjective.

Some quotations have been altered slightly to condense an otherwise bulky or long phrase: a word added or corrected, a phrase deleted, or perhaps punctuation changed. The advantages of so doing include increased brevity, clarity, or general application of the message. The disadvantage, more to the serious scholar than to others, is that in these few cases the quotation does not appear exactly as it does in the original source.

Every effort has been made to preserve the original meaning and the context. Every statement made by General Authorities now living has been submitted to them for their approval before publication.

Gratitude is expressed to Wm. James Mortimer, Lowell Durham, Eleanor Knowles, Emily Bennett, and Michael Graves of Deseret Book for their helpful suggestions and assistance. Thanks, too, must go to David K. Peterson.

Words cannot express my love for my wife, Melanie, and our children, David, Michelle, Michael, and Jared, without whom this project would all have been in vain.

GENERAL AUTHORITIES QUOTED

The following General Authorities are quoted
in *Sentence Sermons*. Dates in parentheses after
each name indicate birthdate (and in some cases
death date, where that date is not the same as the date
indicating end of period of service as a General
Authority), the date of calling as a General Authority,
and the date of death or release from such service.

Joseph Anderson (1889, 1970-)
Marvin J. Ashton (1915, 1969-)
Marvin O. Ashton (1883, 1938-1946)
Melvin J. Ballard (1873, 1919-1939)
William H. Bennett (1910, 1970-)
Adam S. Bennion (1886, 1953-1958)
Samuel O. Bennion (1874, 1933-1945)
Ezra T. Benson (1811, 1846-1869)
Ezra Taft Benson (1899, 1943-)
Albert E. Bowen (1875, 1937-1953)
William R. Bradford (1933, 1975-)
Hugh B. Brown (1883, 1953-1975)
Victor L. Brown (1914, 1961-)
Carl W. Buehner (1898-1974, 1952-1961)
Theodore M. Burton (1907, 1960-)
George Q. Cannon (1827, 1860-1901)
Sylvester Q. Cannon (1877, 1925-1943)
Charles A. Callis (1865, 1933-1947)
ElRay L. Christiansen (1897, 1951-1975)
J. Reuben Clark, Jr. (1871, 1933-1961)
Rudger Clawson (1857, 1898-1943)
Matthew Cowley (1897, 1945-1953)
Matthias F. Cowley (1858-1940, 1897-1905)
William J. Critchlow, Jr. (1892, 1958-1968)
James A. Cullimore (1906, 1966-)
Loren C. Dunn (1930, 1968-)
Paul H. Dunn (1924, 1964-)
Alvin R. Dyer (1903, 1958-1977)
Richard L. Evans (1906, 1938-1971)
James E. Faust (1920, 1972-)

Vaughn J. Featherstone (1931, 1972-)
J. Thomas Fyans (1918, 1974-)
Heber J. Grant (1856, 1882-1945)
Jedediah M. Grant (1816, 1845-1856)
David B. Haight (1906, 1970-)
Robert D. Hales (1932, 1975-)
Marion D. Hanks (1921, 1953-)
Charles H. Hart (1866, 1906-1934)
Alonzo A. Hinckley (1870, 1934-1936)
Gordon B. Hinckley (1910, 1958-)
Howard W. Hunter (1907, 1959-)
Milton R. Hunter (1902, 1945-1975)
Orson Hyde (1805, 1835-1878)
Thorpe B. Isaacson (1898, 1946-1970)
Anthony W. Ivins (1852, 1907-1934)
Antoine R. Ivins (1881, 1931-1967)
Heber C. Kimball (1801, 1835-1868)
J. Golden Kimball (1853, 1892-1938)
Spencer W. Kimball (1895, 1943-)
Harold B. Lee (1899, 1941-1973)
John Longden (1898, 1951-1969)
Anthon H. Lund (1844, 1889-1921)
Francis M. Lyman (1840, 1880-1916)
Richard R. Lyman (1870-1963, 1918-1943)
Bruce R. McConkie (1915, 1946-)
David O. McKay (1873, 1906-1970)
Thomas E. McKay (1875, 1941-1958)
Joseph W. McMurrin (1858, 1897-1932)
Neal A. Maxwell (1926, 1974-)
Joseph F. Merrill (1868, 1931-1952)
Marriner W. Merrill (1832, 1889-1906)
Thomas S. Monson (1927, 1963-)
George Q. Morris (1874, 1951-1962)
Henry D. Moyle (1889, 1947-1963)
Charles W. Nibley (1849, 1907-1931)
Boyd K. Packer (1924, 1961-)
Charles W. Penrose (1832, 1904-1925)
L. Tom Perry (1922, 1972-)
Mark E. Petersen (1900, 1944-)
H. Burke Peterson (1923, 1972-)
Orson Pratt (1811, 1835-1881)
Parley P. Pratt (1807, 1835-1857)

Hartman Rector, Jr. (1924, 1968-)
George Reynolds (1842, 1890-1909)
Charles C. Rich (1809, 1849-1883)
Franklin D. Richards (1821, 1849-1899)
Franklin D. Richards (1900, 1960-)
George F. Richards (1861, 1906-1950)
LeGrand Richards (1886, 1938-)
Stephen L Richards (1879, 1917-1959)
B. H. Roberts (1857, 1888-1933)
Marion G. Romney (1897, 1941-)
Sterling W. Sill (1903, 1954-)
Robert L. Simpson (1915, 1961-)
David A. Smith (1879-1952, 1907-1938)
Eldred G. Smith (1907, 1947-)
George A. Smith (1817, 1839-1875)
George Albert Smith (1870, 1903-1951)
Hyrum G. Smith (1879, 1912-1932)
Hyrum M. Smith (1872, 1901-1918)
John Henry Smith (1848, 1880-1911)
Joseph Smith (1805, 1830-1844)
Joseph F. Smith (1838, 1866-1918)
Joseph Fielding Smith (1876, 1910-1972)
Reed Smoot (1862, 1900-1941)
Erastus Snow (1818, 1849-1888)
Lorenzo Snow (1814, 1849-1901)
Alma Sonne (1884, 1941-1977)
O. Leslie Stone (1903, 1972-)
James E. Talmage (1862, 1911-1933)
N. Eldon Tanner (1898, 1960-)
Henry D. Taylor (1903, 1958-)
John Taylor (1808, 1838-1887)
John W. Taylor (1858-1916, 1884-1905)
George Teasdale (1831, 1882-1907)
Moses Thatcher (1842-1909, 1879-1896)
A. Theodore Tuttle (1919, 1958-)
John H. Vandenberg (1904, 1951-)
Daniel H. Wells (1814, 1857-1891)
John Wells (1864-1941, 1918-1938)
Rulon S. Wells (1854, 1893-1941)
Orson F. Whitney (1855, 1906-1931)
John A. Widtsoe (1872, 1921-1952)
Joseph B. Wirthlin (1917, 1975-)

Joseph L. Wirthlin (1893-1963, 1938-1961)
Abraham O. Woodruff (1872, 1897-1904)
Wilford Woodruff (1807, 1839-1898)
Brigham Young (1801, 1835-1877)
Brigham Young, Jr. (1836, 1864-1903)
Clifford E. Young (1883, 1941-1958)
Joseph Young (1797, 1835-1881)
Levi Edgar Young (1874, 1909-1963)
Seymour B. Young (1837, 1882-1924)
S. Dilworth Young (1897, 1945-)

KEY TO ABBREVIATIONS

ACR   *Area Conference Report.* ACR 8/71 indicates the first area general conference, held in England in August 1971; ACR 8/72, in August 1972 in Mexico; ACR 8/73, in August 1973 in Germany; and ACR 8/74, in August 1974 in Sweden. Area conference reports have not been issued in the English language for subsequent area conferences.

CR   *Conference Report.* A reference to CR 10/31:115, for example, means the *Conference Report* of October 1931, page 115.

HC   *History of the Church,* by Joseph Smith. References in this seven-volume set are listed by volume number and page; for example, HC 6:111 means volume 6, page 111.

JD   *Journal of Discourses.* A reference of JD 1:42 means volume 1, page 42.

ABILITY

We must not let the things we can't do keep us from doing the things we can do.
Richard L. Evans, CR 4/50:105

Life in the Church soon teaches us that the Lord does not ask us about our ability, but only about our availability. And then, if we demonstrate our dependability, the Lord will increase our capability.
Neal A. Maxwell, ACR 8/74:12

I find that the more I do the more ability the Almighty gives me.
Daniel H. Wells, JD 9:83

ADULTERY

If a man commit adultery, he cannot receive the celestial kingdom of God. Even if he is saved in any kingdom, it cannot be the celestial kingdom.
Joseph Smith, HC 6:81

See also: Sex

ADVERSITY

It is not on the pinnacle of success and ease where men and women grow most. It is often down in the valley of heartache and disappointment and reverses where men and women grow into strong characters.
Ezra Taft Benson, ACR 8/74:70

I have been struck with the fact that Deity himself, half mortal for the time, found himself asking that his destiny might be changed, but he finished his petition, "Nevertheless not my will, but thine, be done."
J. Reuben Clark, Jr., CR 10/60:90

Adversity and trial have driven the roots of faith and testimony deep in order to tap the reservoir of spiritual strength that comes from such experiences.
Loren C. Dunn, CR 4/74:36-37

As life supplies its store of tribulation, we need the consolation that comes with knowing that God is good and that he is near, that he understands.
Marion D. Hanks, CR 4/75:16

They who reach down into the depths of life where, in the stillness, the voice of God is heard, have the stabilizing power which carries them poised and serene through the hurricane of difficulties.
Spencer W. Kimball, CR 10/73:149

Just as a flood-lighted temple is more beautiful in a severe storm or in a heavy fog, so the gospel of Jesus Christ is more glorious in times of inward storm and of personal sorrow and tormenting conflict.
Harold B. Lee, CR 4/65:16

There is no development of character without resistance; there is no growth of spirituality without overcoming.
David O. McKay, CR 10/45:133

The winds of tribulation, which blow out some men's candles of commitment, only fan the fires of faith of [others].
Neal A. Maxwell, CR 10/74:15

All of the troubles in the world are born very tiny. They are so tiny that there isn't a one that you couldn't smash between your little fingers. They can grow as big as dinosaurs, but they're always born little.
Boyd K. Packer, ACR 8/71:128

My soul has made its greatest growth as I have been driven to my knees by adversity and affliction.
Marion G. Romney, CR 10/69:60

Difficulty is one of the prices that we pay for our blessings.
Sterling W. Sill, CR 4/70:28

There can be no clouds so dark, so gloomy or so heavy, but God will roll them away in His own time and will

bring good out of threatening evil.
Joseph F. Smith, CR 4/99:41

When the darkness comes, let us remember that the night brings out the stars as sorrows show us the truth; and the insight that comes through pain and disappointment may be the insight into the value of what we are.
Levi Edgar Young, CR 10/32:58-59

I tell you the pathway through adversity is the safest way to heaven. When men get prospered, they get lifted up, and then they lose the Spirit of God.
Joseph Young, JD 6:210

AGENCY

Fate brushes man with its wings, but we make our own fate largely.
Spencer W. Kimball, CR 10/70:72

I never expect to see the day when we shall come to the iron bedstead plan—that if a man be too long for the bedstead he will have to be shortened to fit it; or if he be too short, he will have to be stretched out.
Joseph F. Smith, CR 10/98:23

If a child is besmudged with dirt, we do not let him wait until he grows up to decide whether or not he will bathe.
N. Eldon Tanner, CR 4/73:58

See also: Compulsion, Free Agency, Individuality

AMERICA

America stands in need of the gospel of strenuous work.
Charles A. Callis, CR 10/40:118

The true destiny of America is *religious*, not political; it is *spiritual*, not physical.
Alvin R. Dyer, CR 10/68:106

The united, well-ordered American home is one of the greatest contributing factors to the preservation of the Constitution of the United States.
David O. McKay, CR 4/35:110

The whole of America is Zion itself from north to south.
Joseph Smith, HC 6:318-19

The fetters of tyranny were not stricken from America for the sake of Americans alone.
Orson F. Whitney, CR 4/18:77

See also: Constitution

ANGELS

Gods have an ascendancy over the angels, who are ministering servants. In the resurrection, some are raised to be angels; others are raised to become Gods.
Joseph Smith, HC 5:426-27

ANGER

Whenever you get red in the face, whenever you raise your voice, whenever you get "hot under the collar," or angry, rebellious, or negative in spirit, then know that the spirit of God is leaving you and the spirit of Satan is beginning to take over.
Theodore M. Burton, CR 10/74:77

The longer we are members of the Church, the better we understand the gospel, the more we will be inclined to be peacefully minded. The more diligently we follow the teaching of Christ, the slower we will be to be angry with each other and the quicker we will be to forgive each other.
Theodore M. Burton, ACR 8/73:98

To make decisions while infuriated is as unwise and foolish as it is for a captain to put out to sea in a raging storm.
ElRay L. Christiansen, CR 4/71:27

Shouting is sometimes thought to be a substitute for truth.
  Richard L. Evans, CR 10/41:118

None of us can afford to pay the price of resenting or hating, because of what it does to us.
  Marion D. Hanks, CR 10/73:16

No man has any influence or power for good when angry.
  J. Golden Kimball, CR 4/09:38

Anger itself does more harm than the condition which aroused anger.
  David O. McKay, CR 4/58:5

He who harbors hatred and bitterness injures himself far more than the one towards whom he manifests these evil propensities.
  David O. McKay, CR 10/65:11

A man who cannot control his temper is not very likely to control his passions, and no matter what his pretensions in religion, he moves in daily life very close to the animal plane.
  David O. McKay, CR 10/63:89

If you want to be miserable, just harbor hate for a brother, and if you want to hate, just do your brother some injury. But if you would be happy, render a kind service, make somebody else happy.
  David O. McKay, CR 10/36:104-5

If a spirit of bitterness is in you, don't be in haste.
  Joseph Smith, HC 6:315

I cannot have hatred in my heart for my fellow men, whether they be in the Church or out of it, if I abide in the commandment of the Lord.
  Joseph Fielding Smith, CR 10/20:54

Do not get so angry that you cannot pray: do not allow yourselves to become so angry that you cannot

feed an enemy—even your worst enemy, if an opportunity should present itself.
Brigham Young, JD 5:228

The only vulnerable place in our armor is where we ourselves leave it exposed, because God has armed us at all points. He has made us impervious to outside attacks. But when we boil inside, destruction waits upon us.
Brigham Young, Jr., CR 4/98:26

APOSTASY

Do not wonder at your sons and daughters going astray and losing the faith, when they do not read the word of God.
George Q. Cannon, CR 10/97:40

When you find a man that has fallen by the wayside, you can trace in his course the neglect of some duty or the violation of some covenant which he has made with his God.
Matthias F. Cowley, CR 10/98:9

There is no turning back for a Latter-day Saint, and he who thinks there is, finds himself not turning back but turning away.
Richard L. Evans, CR 10/38:93

That person who thinks he has outgrown his Church and his religion has in reality proved himself too small to bear the responsibilities his membership entails and has shut himself up in his small intellectual world, and the vast treasures in the unseen world of spiritual truths are closed to his understanding.
Harold B. Lee, CR 4/59:68

Men become murmurers or fighters against this Church, for one of two reasons: either through sin— for sin hates truth and virtue—or through ignorance.
David O. McKay, CR 4/09:66

If persons separate themselves from the Lord's Church, they thereby separate themselves from His means of salvation, for salvation is through the Church.
Mark E. Petersen, CR 4/73:159

✦ Personal sin is as much an apostasy from Christ as an acceptance of false doctrines and man-made rituals.
Mark E. Petersen, CR 4/65:35

✦ No man or woman has ever gone astray, or ever will do so, when in full accord with the Presidency of this Church and the Twelve Apostles.
George F. Richards, CR 10/35:30

When the Church as an organization ceased to exist; when that glorious sun set behind the horizon of man's vision it did leave, at least, some lights in the sky that reflected some portions of the truth of the Gospel of Jesus Christ.
B. H. Roberts, CR 4/04:16

Iniquity of any kind cannot be sustained in the Church, and it will not fare well where I am; for I am determined while I do lead the Church, to lead it right.
Joseph Smith, HC 5:411

I will give you one of the keys of the mysteries of the kingdom. It is an eternal principle, that has existed with God from all eternity: That man who rises up to condemn others, finding fault with the Church, saying that they are out of the way, while he himself is righteous, then know assuredly, that that man is in the high road to apostasy; and if he does not repent, will apostatize, as God lives.
Joseph Smith, HC 3:385

If we falter and turn aside, our lamp will burn dim and finally go out, when lo, the Comforter, the source of revelation, will leave us, and darkness will take its place; then how great will be that darkness!
Joseph F. Smith, JD 18:273

There is no one that can get up some foolish idea, or start out proposing to organize a church of some kind, no matter what the inconsistency of his claims may be, but what he will find some one to follow him, somebody as foolish as he is, and who knows as little.
Joseph F. Smith, CR 10/09:9

The danger of our becoming lukewarm is not from without—the danger is within.
Reed Smoot, CR 4/03:55

It will not pay us to apostatize; neither will it pay us to sin. It costs ten thousand times more than it is worth from beginning to end.
Wilford Woodruff, JD 21:318

This Gospel tree which was planted in the meridian of time by Jesus Himself and which was nurtured by Him and His followers, was shorn of many of its limbs and branches to suit the wishes of the ungodly, until its symmetry was lost.
Abraham O. Woodruff, CR 4/04:35

I want to see if I can make some of you apostatize; I will if I can, by teaching sound doctrine and advocating correct principles.
Brigham Young, JD 3:6

 The greater the light bestowed upon an individual or upon a people, the greater the darkness when that light is forsaken.
Brigham Young, JD 8:121

 Omission of duty leads to apostasy.
Brigham Young, JD 11:108

See also: Christianity, False prophets

APPETITE

As the relish with which one enjoys a meal depends upon the appetite he brings to the table more than upon the quality and variety of food placed before

him, so the degree of enjoyment and assimilation of
spiritual refreshment will depend upon whether or not
we "hunger and thirst" as enjoined by the Savior.
    Hugh B. Brown, CR 4/63:6

A person's reaction to his appetites and impulses when
they are aroused gives the measure of that person's
character.
    David O. McKay, CR 4/64:4

A person who indulges his appetites, either secretly or
otherwise, has a character that will not serve him
when he is tempted to indulge his passions.
    David O. McKay, CR 4/68:8

The man who yields to every appetite and every desire
of the flesh cannot receive exaltation, because he does
not prepare himself for and make himself worthy of it.
    Joseph Fielding Smith, CR 4/33:24

    See also: Body, Passions, Self-control

ATHEISM

Atheists do not find God for the same reason that
thieves do not find policemen.
    Anon. Marion D. Hanks, CR 4/66:148

No nation can fully preserve its institutions and
wholly disregard God.
    Melvin J. Ballard, CR 10/29:50

Students for the most part don't learn their atheism
and doctrines of uncertainty from the philosophies
they study in school. These philosophies only make
articulate a latent and unexpressed way of life that
they have learned all too well in the home and from
the society that nurtured them.
    Paul H. Dunn, CR 10/67:125

Atheism is the cause of most of our ills.
    Mark E. Petersen, CR 4/68:60

ATONEMENT

The most significant sacrifice of all, the greatest work ever done for mankind and the turning point in the history of man, is the atonement of Christ, which was a vicarious offering made by Jesus for us who were estranged from God.
  Theodore M. Burton, CR 10/64:35

The principal question before us is not do we comprehend the atonement, but do we accept it.
  George Q. Morris, CR 4/56:112

Through the blood of the Lamb we have amnesty from spiritual death if we keep the commandments of the Lord.
  Boyd K. Packer, CR 4/63:109

  See also: Jesus Christ

BAPTISM

If we are to come into the Church and Kingdom of God it must be by some such means as birth. We must be born into the Kingdom of God. We cannot walk into it; we cannot run or jump into it, or drop into it, or grow up into it; we must be born into it. We must go through the door, and the door is baptism.
  Rudger Clawson, CR 10/30:77

Every Latter-day Saint is born in the Church, and there is only one birth that admits them into the Church, and that is the birth of baptism—the birth of the water and of the Spirit.
  Seymour B. Young, CR 4/03:5

BEHAVIOR

We read a man's character and feelings by his actions.
  Orson Hyde, JD 5:356

Everyone has a set of traits about as characteristic as

his fingerprints, and the best key to his identity is what he does.
  Sterling W. Sill, CR 10/75:44

We can't always control what others think of us, or how others judge us, but we can control the kinds of messages we send out through our behavior.
  O. Leslie Stone, CR 10/75:60

He lives best who thinks best; he acts best, who loves best.
  Levi Edgar Young, CR 4/13:72

BELIEF

He who believes knows that he belongs.
  Marion D. Hanks, CR 4/68:57

To believe is to see.
  Howard W. Hunter, CR 10/62:23

A man may say he believes, but if he does nothing to make that belief or faith a moving power to do, to accomplish, to produce soul growth, his professing will avail him nothing.
  David O. McKay, CR 4/57:7

No man on the earth will ever be saved by the Gospel unless he believes it.
  Hyrum M. Smith, CR 4/04:51

I never hear of a man being damned for believing too much.
  Joseph Smith, HC 6:477

We cannot have faith without belief, but we can believe without having faith.
  O. Leslie Stone, CR 4/73:90

A man is not a bad man because he is not what we call spiritually-minded, quick to believe in the marvelous, in spiritual mysteries and manifestations. The world is made up of two great classes of

people—the spiritually-minded and the
worldly-minded; and even among the former class
some believe more readily than others.
Orson F. Whitney, CR 4/11:48

See also: Faith, Testimony

BENEVOLENCE

Everyone may not be beneficent, but all may be
benevolent.
David O. McKay, CR 10/52:10

Benevolence in its fullest sense is the sum of moral
excellence, and comprehends every other virtue.
David O. McKay, CR 4/68:8

BIBLE

If it is old-fashioned to believe in the Bible, we should
thank God for the privilege of being old-fashioned.
Howard W. Hunter, CR 10/70:132

There are no people on the earth that quibble so little
about the Bible as do the Latter-day Saints.
J. Golden Kimball, CR 4/03:31

Our latitude and longitude can be determined in the
original Hebrew with far greater accuracy than in the
English version.
Joseph Smith, HC 5:342-43

From sundry revelations which had been received, it
was apparent that many important points touching
the salvation of man, had been taken from the Bible,
or lost before it was compiled.
Joseph Smith, HC 1:245

I believe the Bible as it read when it came from the
pen of the original writers. Ignorant translators,
careless transcribers, or designing and corrupt priests
have committed many errors.
Joseph Smith, HC 6:57

I have an old edition of the New Testament in the Latin, Hebrew, German and Greek languages. I have been reading the German, and find it to be the most correct translation, and to correspond nearest to the revelations which God has given to me for the last fourteen years.
Joseph Smith, HC 6:307

> *See also:* Scripture

BIRTH

The Spirits of men are being born into the world by divine appointment, and not by accident.
Joseph W. McMurrin, CR 4/04:67

> *See also:* Mortality

BLESSINGS

A blessing always carries with it a responsibility.
J. Reuben Clark, Jr., CR 10/54:38

There is no blessing that the Latter-day Saints need that they may not enjoy.
George Albert Smith, CR 10/08:83

If others' blessings are not your blessings, others' curses are not your curses.
Joseph Smith, HC 1:283

Blessings offered, but rejected, are no longer blessings.
Joseph Smith, HC 5:135

BODY

Your body becomes an instrument of your mind and the foundation of your character.
Boyd K. Packer, CR 4/73:79

Any conscious, wilful impairment of the body is an affront to God.
Stephen L Richards, CR 10/36:30

Next to the human spirit the human body is the most marvelous of God's creations.
Sterling W. Sill, CR 4/63:42

Through the body the experiences of earth are made the possession of the spirit.
John A. Widtsoe, CR 4/26:108

See also: Appetites

BOOK OF MORMON

No man had yet so much as heard of the Book of Mormon but what the Spirit of the Lord whispered quietly to his soul that that book was true.
B. H. Roberts, CR 4/05:44

I told the brethren that the Book of Mormon was the most correct of any book on earth, and the keystone of our religion, and a man would get nearer to God by abiding by its precepts, than by any other book.
Joseph Smith, HC 4:461

Take away the Book of Mormon and the revelations, and where is our religion?
Joseph Smith, HC 2:52

No member of this Church can stand approved in the presence of God who has not seriously and carefully read the Book of Mormon.
Joseph Fielding Smith, CR 10/61:18

See also: Scripture

BROAD-MINDEDNESS

Broad-mindedness too often is nothing but a flattening out of high-mindedness!
Hugh B. Brown, CR 4/70:77

BROTHERHOOD

How can a man have communion with God if he does

not have fellowship with his fellow men?
Hugh B. Brown, CR 4/63:8

See also: Friendship

CELESTIAL KINGDOM

The celestial kingdom is a central college where all
true sciences exist.
Orson Hyde, JD 15:304

There is no shortage of room in the celestial kingdom.
Boyd K. Packer, CR 4/75:157

There is no power in the universe that can come
between us and the celestial kingdom, except our own
power.
Sterling W. Sill, CR 10/75:42

CEMETERIES

The place where a man is buried is sacred to me.
Joseph Smith, HC 5:361

Whenever a man of God is in a place where many
have been killed, he will feel lonesome and
unpleasant, and his spirits will sink.
Joseph Smith, HC 2:66

See also: Death

CHARACTER

Character is the one thing we make in this world and
take with us into the next.
Ezra Taft Benson, CR 4/66:128

Real character is formed in the midst of the battles for
the soul.
Hugh B. Brown, CR 4/64:55

The observance of divine instructions is the most

effective means for the best development of men and women.
Sylvester Q. Cannon, CR 10/29:44

A true measure of one's devotion to a principle is measured not by what he professes, but by what he manifests—day by day.
ElRay L. Christiansen, CR 10/52:55

If we are building upon the foundation which our pioneer fathers laid for us here, we will not build better buildings; we will build better characters.
Matthew Cowley, CR 4/47:37

Abstract qualities of character don't mean much in the abstract.
Richard L. Evans, CR 4/66:89

We can run away from where we are, but not from what we are.
Richard L. Evans, CR 4/54:85

No man can rise above the limitations of his own character.
Richard L. Evans, CR 4/57:12

Character is an achievement, not a gift.
Marion D. Hanks, CR 4/68:55

We read a man's character and feelings by his actions.
Orson Hyde, JD 5:356

Character certainly is worth more than education without it.
Richard R. Lyman, CR 4/23:155

The foundation of a noble character is integrity.
David O. McKay, CR 4/64:6

Man cannot escape for one moment the radiation of his character.
David O. McKay, CR 10/69:87

A person's reaction to his appetites and impulses when

they are aroused gives the measure of that person's character.
  David O. McKay, CR 4/64:4

Every person radiates what he or she is. Every person is a recipient of radiation.
  David O. McKay, CR 4/63:129

Flabbiness of character more than flabbiness of muscles lies at the root of most of the problems facing American youth.
  David O. McKay, CR 4/59:72

The character of a child is formed largely during the first twelve years of his life.
  David O. McKay, CR 10/51:10

No permanent success comes to those who do not possess good character.
  Stephen L Richards, CR 10/52:101

The greatest responsibility that is ever entrusted to any human being is that of building his own personality.
  Sterling W. Sill, CR 4/62:13

The real worth of a man is not in himself alone, but in what he stands for.
  Sterling W. Sill, CR 4/54:118

Character is determined by the extent to which we can master ourselves toward good ends.
  N. Eldon Tanner, CR 4/75:111

We want no flabbiness of character when spiritual strength is required.
  A. Theodore Tuttle, CR 10/74:100

The success of this life is not measured at the end of it by what we have, but rather by what we are.
  Rulon S. Wells, CR 10/12:25

If you were in possession of all the wealth in the world, it is not worth so much to you as your good characters.
Brigham Young, JD 8:346

The social security of a nation is based on the character of the citizens, not on the amount of material comforts the government may bestow upon them.
Levi Edgar Young, CR 10/36:68

CHARITY

We may be charitable and forbearing to the sinner, but must condemn the sin.
David O. McKay, CR 10/39:102

In essentials let there be unity; in non-essentials, liberty; and in all things, charity.
B. H. Roberts, CR 10/12:30

A man filled with the love of God, is not content with blessing his family alone, but ranges through the whole world, anxious to bless the whole human race.
Joseph Smith, HC 4:227

Rather spare ten iniquitous among you, than condemn one innocent one.
Joseph Smith, HC 5:21

See also: Love

CHASTISEMENT

Every man in the world who gives blows must take blows, and until a man becomes as good an anvil as he is a hammer he fails to be thoroughly fitted for his work.
Anon. J. Golden Kimball, CR 4/05:53

If you are ever called upon to chasten a person, never chasten beyond the balm you have within you to bind up.
Brigham Young, JD 9:124-25

CHASTITY

As long as the stars shine in the heavens and the sun brings warmth to the earth and so long as men and women live upon this earth, there must be this holy standard of chastity and virtue.
Spencer W. Kimball, ACR 8/74:10

The test of true womanhood comes when the woman stands innocent at the court of chastity.
David O. McKay, CR 4/67:8

A chaste, not a profligate life is the source of virile manhood, the crown of beautiful womanhood, the contributing source of harmony and happiness in family life, and the source of strength and perpetuity of the race.
David O. McKay, CR 10/51:9

Chastity, not indulgence, during pre-marital years, is the source of harmony and happiness in the home, and the chief contributing factor to the health and perpetuity of the race.
David O. McKay, CR 4/43:20-21

No one can transgress the laws of chastity and find peace.
David O. McKay, CR 10/20:44

Humanity will rise or fall through its attitude toward the law of chastity.
Mark E. Petersen, CR 4/69:62

See also: Morality, Virtue

CHILDREN

Your children . . . are like diamonds. True, they may need polish, in order to bring out their brilliancy and best qualities; and education of the right kind will impart this lustre.
George Q. Cannon, JD 22:276

The most important consideration with reference to children would be the question of environment— environment of the home first, and environment of the church second.
Rudger Clawson, CR 10/07:28

Parents are deceiving themselves in imagining that their children will be born with a knowledge of the Gospel.
Heber J. Grant, CR 4/02:80

Children are like the flowers of God, and they must have time and room to bloom.
Thorpe B. Isaacson, CR 10/63:97

Most ills of life are due to failure of parents to teach their children and the failure of posterity to listen.
Spencer W. Kimball, ACR 8/74:48

Children . . . will never go astray while they are in good company.
Francis M. Lyman, CR 10/07:15

Our most precious possessions are not our abundant harvests, nor our orchards yielding luscious fruit, nor our waterways, nor our million miles of paved highways, nor our oil wells, nor our rich mines of copper, silver and gold, nor even of uranium—our most precious possessions, our treasures of eternity, are our children.
David O. McKay, CR 10/54:8

The laughter of little children is music in the well-ordered home.
David O. McKay, CR 4/30:82

There are three fundamental things to which every child is entitled. First, a respected name; second, a sense of security; third, opportunities for development.
David O. McKay, CR 4/35:113

Those who do too much *for* their children will soon find they can do nothing *with* their children. So many

children have been so much *done for* they are almost *done in.*
    Neal A. Maxwell, CR 4/75:150

Each time a child is born, the world somehow is renewed in innocence.
    Boyd K. Packer, ACR 8/74:83

The failure of parents to teach their children affects not only them and their children but whole civilizations.
    Marion G. Romney, CR 4/69:108

There is nothing more precious to us than our children and our eternal happiness will be largely conditioned by what they attain to.
    George Albert Smith, CR 4/39:124

Only out of purposeful, divine relationship of parent and child grows eternal joy and fulfillment.
    A. Theodore Tuttle, CR 10/72:70

If we lose our children in the process of attaining exaltation, I think it is a little vain to assume that we are going to have very much happiness.
    S. Dilworth Young, CR 4/58:31

Satan may have no power to tempt a child before eight years of age, but some of his emissaries go all out to condition a child so that when he becomes eight he will not be conscious that sinning is very bad.
    S. Dilworth Young, CR 4/55:99

    See also: Family, Parents, Youth

CHRIST (See Jesus Christ)

CHRISTIANITY

The measure of a man's Christianity may be determined by the way he gets and spends his money.
    Anon. Stephen L Richards, CR 4/29:50

To fail to honor that royal name we bear as Christians is to hold the very God we espouse to open ridicule and shame.
Theodore M. Burton, CR 4/70:92

Christianity as it was practiced through the centuries fostered kingdoms rather than replaced them.
Theodore M. Burton, CR 4/71:108

True Christianity is Love in action.
David O. McKay, CR 10/49:119

Real Christianity is contagious.
Neal A. Maxwell, CR 4/75:149

The Christian religion cannot be separated from the Christian life.
Mark E. Petersen, CR 10/66:106

Where there is no mortality, there is no true Christianity.
Mark E. Petersen, CR 4/65:36

A Christian brotherhood can no more be built without the acceptance of the fact that Jesus is the Son of God than the superstructure of [a] great building can be supported without its foundation.
Marion G. Romney, CR 4/55:32

See also: Apostasy, Religion

CHURCH

I am more interested in seeing the truth succeed than any organization to which I belong, but thank God, the organization to which I belong has the truth.
Melvin J. Ballard, CR 4/32:61

The Church is for man, not man for the Church.
Ezra Taft Benson, CR 10/45:160

The church must be judged by what it is, not by what people say of it.
Anthony W. Ivins, CR 10/23:143

The power of the Church is in the administration of
the priesthood offices.
Antoine R. Ivins, CR 10/60:106

God save the people, for if it were not for the people,
we would not need this great Church.
J. Golden Kimball, CR 4/24:70

Let us be pioneers (for our people yet to be born) by
planting the wheat of our witness, that those who
follow us may eat of the bread of belief in time of
famine elsewhere in the world!
Spencer W. Kimball, CR 4/76:70

The strength of the Church is not in the numbers, nor
in the amount of tithes and offerings paid by faithful
members, nor in the magnitude of chapels and temple
buildings, but because in the hearts of faithful
members of the Church is the conviction that this is
indeed the church and kingdom of God on the earth.
Harold B. Lee, CR 4/73:9

Our religion is not a cloak to wear on Sunday and be
hung in the closet for the rest of the week; neither is it
something for nations to parade on certain occasions
and then to wrap up in mothballs to await another
occasion.
David O. McKay, CR 4/62:125

The strength of this Church lies in the purity of the
thoughts and lives of its workers.
David O. McKay, CR 10/58:91-92

The great purpose of the Church is to translate truth
into a better social order.
David O. McKay, CR 10/66:85

The Church does not tear down the houses of others,
before erecting one that is more commodious and
more beautiful.
David O. McKay, CR 4/09:64

The real test of any Church or religion is the kind of
men it makes.
David O. McKay, CR 4/49:11

The Church helps us to achieve things that we simply could not achieve if we were left alone with our random impulses to do good.
Neal A. Maxwell, ACR 8/74:13

There is no need for any person in this Church to have an empty mind, an empty hand, or an empty heart.
George Q. Morris, CR 4/52:31

When everything else passes away like the dream of a night vision, this Church, this kingdom, will go on to its decreed destiny.
LeGrand Richards, CR 4/74:171

The genius of our Church government is government through *councils.*
Stephen L Richards, CR 10/53:86

For my own part the Church is my union, the Church is my club, the Church is my lodge, the Church is my fraternity; and I want to say to every man that there is within the Church an opportunity for the expression of every legitimate desire that should be in the heart of men.
Stephen L Richards, CR 10/19:103

I know nothing about the Church that is perfect, excepting only the plan itself which is God-given.
Stephen L Richards, CR 10/38:116

As I understand the Church of Christ its mission is twofold: first, it is to proclaim the truth; second, it is to perfect those who receive the truth.
B. H. Roberts, CR 10/03:75

We are connected with an institution founded of God for the benefit of the whole world, and it is an institution of world-wide sympathies.
B. H. Roberts, CR 4/07:59

Joseph Smith was great; but great as he was, rising up and towering far above him is the work that he accomplished through divine guidance; that work is

infinitely greater than the prophet—greater than all
the prophets connected with it.
  B. H. Roberts, CR 10/03:74

While the Church of Jesus Christ of Latter-day Saints
is given a prominent part in this great drama of the
last days, it is not the only force nor the only means
that the Lord has employed to bring to pass those
things of which his prophets in ancient times have
testified.
  B. H. Roberts, CR 4/02:14

This Church is the Lord's appointed custodian and
legal administrator of the ordinances of his gospel.
  Marion G. Romney, CR 4/65:105

The organization of the Church is as perfect as it can
possibly be in our present state.
  Hyrum M. Smith, CR 4/02:22

I will take shelter under the broad cover of the wings
of the work in which I am engaged. It matters not to
me if all Hell boils over.
  Joseph Smith, HC 6:253

God's work and His Church will grow and increase
just as fast as we, the members of it, are capable of
carrying out the instructions of God.
  Reed Smoot, CR 4/15:93

The purpose of the Church is to heal, not to spread
disease; to build up, not to tear down; to save, not to
destroy, but that does not mean that we are to look
upon sin in our midst in any namby-pamby way and
pass it by.
  James E. Talmage, CR 10/20:62

Our mission to the world is a mission of peace.
  John Taylor, JD 23:263-64

We are now enjoying the very things that Prophets
prophesied of as they looked through the dark vista of
ages unborn and contemplated these blessings that we
enjoy.
  John Taylor, JD 5:264

The Lord has placed upon the Latter-day Saints three great duties. One is that they shall save themselves; another, that they shall warn the world; and the third, that they shall redeem their dead.
John Wells, CR 10/24:50

The two great gifts to this Church are the gifts of truth and authority.
John A. Widtsoe, CR 4/21:38

Our religion is against everything in the nature of treason, disloyalty, anarchy or rebellion.
Orson F. Whitney, CR 10/07:52

See also: Gospel Plan, Mormonism, Religion

CITIZENSHIP

A citizen who loves justice and hates evil is better than a battleship.
David O. McKay, CR 4/65:8

A man cannot be a good Latter-day Saint and not be a good citizen.
Charles W. Nibley, CR 4/17:142

A good citizen in the Church of God is a good citizen in any good government on the face of the earth.
Stephen L Richards, CR 4/20:99

A great nation can no more exist without good homes than it can exist without the loyalty and patriotism of a devoted citizenship.
Stephen L Richards, CR 4/17:139

There can never be a great citizenship that comes from the mere force, external force of law. You cannot superimpose the duties of citizenship in order to make a great people.
Stephen L Richards, CR 10/19:103

See also: Governments

CIVIL RIGHTS

There is nothing wrong with civil rights; it is what's being done in the name of civil rights that is alarming.
Ezra Taft Benson, CR 10/67:35

CIVILIZATION

When we destroy the principles of honesty, integrity, and morality, our civilization is most certainly on the verge of losing the power to preserve itself.
Joseph Anderson, CR 4/75:45

A civilization is marked by its attitude toward the aged.
Marvin O. Ashton, CR 10/44:105

Good citizens are necessary to civilization, but good parents are obligatory if civilization is to continue.
Thorpe B. Isaacson, CR 4/59:64

Our very civilization is in jeopardy. If it is to be rescued, it must be done by men of integrity.
Marion G. Romney, CR 10/74:103

There can be no true, perfect civilization where there is not faithful obedience to the commandments of God.
Joseph Fielding Smith, CR 4/35:96

The real test of the strength of civilization is in the moral capacity of the rank and file of the citizens to give up the pleasure of the present for greater rewards in the future.
Levi Edgar Young, CR 10/36:67-68

See also: Society, World

COMMANDMENTS

The commandments of the Lord are not dictums, they are principles given by a Merciful Father to keep us

and all mankind who will follow him from sin, sorrow, and regret.
ElRay L. Christiansen, CR 4/63:70

It was never intended that the commandments of God should meet the convenience or the appetites or inclinations of everyone.
Richard L. Evans, CR 10/65:42

I believe that as circumstances change, the Lord changes his commandments, to correspond therewith.
Charles W. Penrose, CR 10/21:17

The Lord does not ask impossibilities of us.
George Reynolds, CR 10/98:19

Every single commandment, stern as it may appear to some, is in reality an avenue to the glorious realm of peace and happiness.
Stephen L Richards, CR 4/56:90

Because we are breaking the Ten Commandments, the Ten Commandments are also breaking us.
Sterling W. Sill, CR 10/71:99

When a man confesses that it is hard to keep the commandments of the Lord, he is making a sad confession: that he is a violator of the gospel law.
Joseph Fielding Smith, CR 4/68:11

It's not nearly so hard to live the commandments as not to live them.
A. Theodore Tuttle, CR 10/65:32

See also: Law

COMMUNICATION

Sin comes when communication lines are down—it always does, sooner or later.
Spencer W. Kimball, CR 4/72:29

There is a form of communication that transcends the power of words.
Joseph B. Wirthlin, CR 10/75:155

See also: Language

COMMUNISM

The degree of a man's aversion to communism may not always be measured by the noise he makes in going about and calling everyone a communist who disagrees with his personal political bias.
Hugh B. Brown, CR 4/62:89

Communism is Satan's counterfeit for the United Order.
J. Reuben Clark, Jr., CR 10/43:11

See also: Governments

COMPULSION

There is no compulsion in any part of the gospel.
Spencer W. Kimball, CR 4/74:125

Compulsion is not a principle of the Gospel of Salvation.
Hyrum M. Smith, CR 10/16:90

God would not exert any compulsory means, and the devil could not.
Joseph Smith, HC 4:358

It is impossible for any man to commit sin under compulsion, and it is impossible for him to do good under compulsion.
Rulon S. Wells, CR 4/41:74

There can be no salvation in compulsion.
Rulon S. Wells, CR 4/30:69

CONFESSION

So long as we put off either the forsaking or confessing of our sins, just so long do we delay the day of our redemption.
Marion G. Romney, CR 10/55:125

No member of the Church stands on ground more firm than the man who has had the courage to unburden himself to his priesthood authority and so set things in order with his Master.
Robert L. Simpson, CR 4/72:32

Satan has spread the false rumor that confidences are rarely kept.
Robert L. Simpson, CR 4/72:33

If you were to relate your private faults to one another, it would tend to injure you; it would weaken and not strengthen either the speaker or the hearer, and would give the enemy more power.
Brigham Young, JD 8:361

See also: Forgiveness, Repentance

CONFIDENCE

Confidence comes through sincere prayer.
David O. McKay, CR 4/22:65

A man can have no greater incentive, no greater hope, no greater strength than to know his mother, his sweetheart, or his wife has confidence in him and loves him.
N. Eldon Tanner, CR 10/73:125

CONSCIENCE

Live so as to have a quiet conscience.
Richard L. Evans, CR 4/54:85

That man is not at peace who is untrue to the

whisperings of Christ—the promptings of his
conscience.
David O. McKay, CR 10/65:10

My conscience condemns me when I do that which is
wrong, and thus rob myself of that peace, happiness
and hope I might have by answering strictly the
requirements of conscience.
George F. Richards, CR 10/14:81

A God-given conscience will not let us rest until our
duty is done.
Robert L. Simpson, CR 10/64:96

The approval of a man's own conscience is his richest
earthly reward.
John Henry Smith, CR 10/10:9

Those who have done wrong always have that wrong
gnawing them.
Joseph Smith, HC 6:366

See also: Holy Ghost

CONSTITUTION

We need the Constitution and its guarantees of liberty
and freedom more than any other people in the world,
for, few and weak as we are, we stand naked and
helpless except when clothed with its benign
provisions.
J. Reuben Clark, Jr., CR 4/35:94

One of the most important things that we can do for
the Church is to stand behind the Constitution of the
United States.
J. Reuben Clark, Jr., CR 4/35:94

Next to being one in worshiping God there is nothing
in this world upon which this Church should be more
united than in upholding and defending the
Constitution of the United States.
David O. McKay, CR 10/39:105

The Constitution of the United States is a glorious standard; it is founded in the wisdom of God. It is a heavenly banner; it is to all those who are privileged with the sweets of its liberty, like the cooling shades and refreshing waters of a great rock in a thirsty and weary land. It is like a great tree under whose branches men from every clime can be shielded from the burning rays of the sun.
Joseph Smith, HC 3:304

The only fault I find with the Constitution is, it is not broad enough to cover the whole ground.
Joseph Smith, HC 6:57

See also: America, Governments

CONTENTION

The evil of being puffed up with correct (though useless) knowledge is not so great as the evil of contention.
Joseph Smith, HC 5:340

The truth will never divide councils of the priesthood. It will never divide Presidents from their Counselors, nor Counselors from their Presidents, nor members of the Church from one another, nor from the Church.
Joseph F. Smith, CR 4/07:4

You find the spirit of contention only among apostates and those who have denied the faith.
Joseph F. Smith, CR 4/08:7

CONVERSION

Salesmanship methods of themselves alone as applied to the teaching of the Gospel will convince the mind but do not convert the heart.
Harold B. Lee, CR 10/60:17

We plant, we labor, we exhort and do our duty, bearing the priesthood; but it is the Lord that gives

the result that causes the convictions and brings about the conversions and the reformations.
Francis M. Lyman, CR 10/09:14

When a soul is brought into a knowledge of the truth and baptized into the fold, that soul is just as precious in the sight of the Lord as is a Prophet, an Apostle, a President, or any other man, for he is a Son of God.
Francis M. Lyman, CR 10/06:17

Conversion is an individual matter.
George Q. Morris, CR 10/54:96

The mark of real conversion is *endurance*.
Hartman Rector, Jr., CR 4/74:161

You must be a convert before you can be a disciple.
Sterling W. Sill, CR 4/73:144

Conversion from a condition of sin and unbelief to one of understanding and faith is not brought about instantaneously.
Hyrum M. Smith, CR 4/06:48

We must have a change of heart to see the kingdom of God, and subscribe to the articles of adoption to enter therein.
Joseph Smith, HC 6:58

That man that has none of the blood of Abraham (naturally) must have a new creation by the Holy Ghost.
Joseph Smith, HC 3:380

See also: Rebirth

COUNSEL

The path of counsel is the path of safety.
George Q. Cannon, JD 13:370

No man is so wise that he cannot benefit by talking things out with others.
Richard L. Evans, CR 4/70:16

None of us—at any age—is ever so old or so young, so knowledgeable or so self-assured, that he doesn't need counsel.
   Richard L. Evans, CR 4/68:85

The Latter-day Saint never goes astray when he relies upon counsel.
   Francis M. Lyman, CR 10/15:76

Advise with those who have wisdom and experience, before you leap lest you leap into the dark.
   Joseph F. Smith, CR 4/10:7

It requires more energy and more strength of purpose in a man to follow out the counsel of one who is just above him than it is to follow a man that is a long way ahead of him.
   Lorenzo Snow, JD 5:315

Nine-tenths of the mistakes of this people would be corrected in the young if they would listen to the counsels of their fathers and mothers.
   John W. Taylor, CR 4/99:62

Do you know why some men give counsel different one from another? Because they undertake to give counsel without the spirit of the Lord to dictate them.
   Brigham Young, JD 5:329

COUNTERFEIT

All good things are counterfeited.
   Rulon S. Wells, CR 10/31:66

The more exalted and glorious the attribute is, the more contemptible and vicious is its counterfeit.
   Rulon S. Wells, CR 10/31:65

COURAGE

Courage is acting in spite of fear.
   Howard W. Hunter, CR 4/67:117

COURTS

No person through the discerning of spirits can bring a charge against another, they must be proven guilty by positive evidence, or they stand clear.
Joseph Smith, HC 4:581

See also: Excommunication

COURTSHIP

During courtship we should keep our eyes wide open, but after marriage keep them half-shut.
David O. McKay, CR 4/56:9

COVETOUSNESS

The man who sets his heart upon the things of the world, who does not hesitate to cheat his brother, who will lie for gain, who will steal from his neighbor, or, who, by slander, will rob another of his reputation, lives on a low, animal plane of existence, and either stifles his spirituality or permits it to lie dormant.
David O. McKay, CR 4/58:7

Unwarrantable installment buying is a pit into which those who covet fall.
John H. Vandenberg, CR 10/66:68

This is my Scripture: They who long and lust after the fashions of the world are destitute of the Spirit of God.
Brigham Young, JD 14:18

COWARDICE

Cowardice, in the end, always brings regret and remorse.
Marion G. Romney, CR 4/75:109

God never called upon cowards to do work for him.
Levi Edgar Young, CR 4/21:171

CREATION

Incomprehensibly grand as are the physical creations of the earth and space, they have been brought into existence as a means to an end; *they* are the handiwork of God; *man* is his son.
    Hugh B. Brown, CR 10/66:105

When God created man in his own image, he did not divest himself of that image.
    Hugh B. Brown, CR 4/69:51

The planetary orbs which stud our heavens so gloriously are peopled by the principle of procreation.
    George Q. Cannon, CR 4/99:20

The earth was created for man and not man for the earth.
    David O. McKay, CR 10/69:6

Anything created cannot be eternal.
    Joseph Smith, HC 3:387

God never had the power to create the spirit of man at all. God himself could not create himself.
    Joseph Smith, HC 6:311

    See also: Man

CREDIT

There is no measure to the good a man may do if he does not worry as to who gets the credit for it.
    Anon. Antoine R. Ivins, CR 4/46:42

No man loses credit by being true to his principles.
    George Q. Cannon, JD 18:12

There's no credit buying on eternal things, none at all. Anything that is worthwhile has to be paid for in advance.
    Boyd K. Packer, ACR 8/71:128

Satan . . . was more concerned with credit than with results.
N. Eldon Tanner, CR 10/75:115

See also: Debt

CREDULITY

It never ceases to amaze me how gullible some of our Church members are.
Harold B. Lee, CR 10/72:126

Credulity is no more like faith than lust, another devilish counterfeit, is like love.
Rulon S. Wells, CR 10/29:31

See also: Faith

CRIME

Avarice and selfishness mastermind all sin and crime.
John H. Vandenberg, CR 10/65:131

Ignorance is the mother of crime.
Abraham O. Woodruff, CR 4/02:79

See also: Sin, Transgression

CRITICISM

The more perfect one becomes, the less he is inclined to speak of the imperfections of others.
ElRay L. Christiansen, CR 4/56:114

You never would complain of the sharpness of the work of God, if you were not under transgression.
Heber C. Kimball, JD 5:173

When it really does become necessary to say things that seem harsh, I always believe in saying them in the very pleasantest manner possible.
B. H. Roberts, CR 10/09:102

I am afraid of the Latter-day Saints getting into a
form of religion and being no better off than their
neighbors, or getting into the habit of going to
meeting and hearing the singing and praying and the
discourse without their having any influence whatever
upon their minds any more than perchance to
criticise.
   George Teasdale, JD 26:50

   See also: Fault-finding

DAMNATION

Men were not created to be damned; but they were
created to be saved.
   Francis M. Lyman, CR 10/98:45

Damnation is no part of the Gospel of Christ. There is
no damnation in it, but there is plenty of damnation
outside of it.
   Orson F. Whitney, CR 4/08:86

DEATH

There was in all earth's area, not one empty grave. No
human heart believed; no human voice declared that
there was such a grave—a grave robbed by the power
of a Victor stronger than man's great enemy, Death.
   Anon. David O. McKay, CR 4/66:56

There is no untimely passing of a prophet of God.
   Ezra Taft Benson, CR 4/74:151

Death is, in the eternal plan, co-equal with birth.
   J. Reuben Clark, Jr., CR 10/40:17

Resolve to live better hereafter so that we can die
better.
   Thorpe B. Isaacson, CR 10/59:97

While mortals mourn "a man is dead," angels
proclaim "a child is born."
   Heber C. Kimball, JD 12:180

Death, but a sleep, is followed by a glorious
awakening in the morning of an eternal realm.
   David O. McKay, CR 4/68:5

Mortal death is no more an ending than birth was a
beginning.
   Boyd K. Packer, CR 10/75:147

Nobody gets out of this life alive.
   Hartman Rector, Jr., CR 10/70:74

Death is an important part of eternal life.
   Franklin D. Richards (1900, 1960-   ), CR 10/72:84

Death is the gateway to immortality. The most
important part of life is death.
   Sterling W. Sill, CR 10/58:105

The chief characteristic of eternal death is not
oblivion but endless pain and regret.
   Sterling W. Sill, CR 4/65:88

The Lord takes many away, even in infancy, that they
may escape the envy of man, and the sorrows and evils
of this present world; they were too pure, too lovely, to
live on earth.
   Joseph Smith, HC 4:553

The only difference between the old and young dying
is, one lives longer in heaven and eternal light and
glory than the other, and is freed a little sooner from
this miserable wicked world.
   Joseph Smith, HC 4:554

There is nothing else quite so sure as that we will one
day leave this frail existence.
   N. Eldon Tanner, CR 10/66:49

   See also: Mortality

DEBT

Let us avoid debt as we would avoid a plague; where

we are now in debt let us get out of debt; if not today, then tomorrow.
J. Reuben Clark, Jr., CR 4/37:26

An honest man is in hell when he is in debt.
J. Golden Kimball, CR 10/31:56

A man cannot be comfortable spiritually who is in bondage financially.
Francis M. Lyman, CR 10/04:18

No man has the right to live beyond his means.
Richard R. Lyman, CR 4/21:144

The easiest and shortest way to get out of debt is to first pay our tithing, promptly and honestly.
Marriner W. Merrill, CR 4/03:66

Just five words spell prosperity, success and happiness—five words only—and they are these: "spend less than you get."
Charles W. Nibley, CR 10/25:14

Credit is a shadow, and debt is bondage.
George A. Smith, JD 17:82

I tell you that to an honest man there is no bondage controlled by human laws upon the face of the earth greater than the bondage of debt.
Reed Smoot, CR 10/00:6

It is impossible for anyone to borrow himself out of debt.
John H. Vandenberg, CR 10/66:68

DECISIONS

When you do take the wrong course, you are undoing the work of your prior existence.
ElRay L. Christiansen, CR 4/74:35

To make decisions while infuriated is as unwise and

foolish as it is for a captain to put out to sea in a raging storm.
ElRay L. Christiansen, CR 4/71:27

Split-second decisions, which all of us sometimes have to make, can be more safely made if there have been set up beforehand some "musts" and some "must nots."
ElRay L. Christiansen, CR 4/58:36

The course of our lives is not determined by great, awesome decisions. Our direction is set by the little day-to-day choices which chart the track on which we run.
Gordon B. Hinckley, CR 10/72:106

If you have not done so yet, decide to decide.
Spencer W. Kimball, CR 4/76:70

To be valiant in the testimony of Jesus is to take the Lord's side on every issue.
Bruce R. McConkie, CR 10/74:46

Every major decision should be made on the basis of the effect it will have on the family unit.
Bruce R. McConkie, CR 4/70:27

Our decisions, once executed, can never be erased. This is because such selections introduce a new series of conditions setting in motion events which cannot later be recalled.
Henry D. Moyle, CR 4/59:98

You can make every decision in your life correctly if you can learn to follow the guidance of the Holy Spirit.
Marion G. Romney, CR 10/61:60

When one has definitely eliminated those things that he will *not* do, then he can concentrate all of his time and energy on the things that he *should* do.
Sterling W. Sill, CR 10/71:97

The mind of man must first depend upon quality

input before it can be counted upon to render good decisions.
  Robert L. Simpson, CR 10/72:144

If a spirit of bitterness is in you, don't be in haste.
  Joseph Smith, HC 6:315

The way to get along in any important matter is to gather unto yourselves wise men, experienced and aged men, to assist in council in all times of trouble.
  Joseph Smith, HC 5:389

It is too late if we wait until the moment of temptation before making our decision.
  N. Eldon Tanner, CR 10/71:137

  See also: Agency, Free Agency

DESIRE

The great human advances have not been brought about by mediocre men and women; they have been achieved by distinctly uncommon people with vital sparks of desire.
  Paul H. Dunn, CR 10/68:53-54

When we really WANT to be disciples of Christ, in capital letters, when we really want to be servants of the Master, then everything else will be easy.
  Sterling W. Sill, CR 4/73:145

Temptations without imply desires within.
  Sterling W. Sill, CR 4/70:29-30

  See also: Intentions, Thoughts

DIGNITY

True dignity is never won by place, and it is never lost when honors are withdrawn.
  Hugh B. Brown, CR 4/70:77

  See also: Self-respect

DISCIPLINE

No system can long command the loyalties of man that does not expect of them certain measures of discipline, and particularly of self-discipline.
Gordon B. Hinckley, CR 4/73:73

Only the unwise foolishly indulge their sons and withhold proper discipline.
A. Theodore Tuttle, CR 10/73:88

Spiritual discipline is the most effective means of character development.
John H. Vandenberg, CR 10/63:48

See also: Self-control

DISCOURSES (See Speaking)

DISHONESTY

It is impossible to associate manhood with dishonesty.
David O. McKay, CR 4/68:7

No man can be dishonest within himself without deadening the susceptibility of his spirit.
David O. McKay, CR 10/29:15

If we allow dishonesty to weave itself into the fabric of our lives, we invite moral suicide.
Mark E. Petersen, CR 10/66:105

DISPENSATION

The candle which the Lord has lighted in this dispensation can become as a light unto the whole world.
Gordon B. Hinckley, CR 10/74:145

The prophetic glass before the eyes of the ancient seers brings the rays of Jehovah's power to a focus on this earth, in these our days.
Orson Hyde, JD 6:49

43

The fire of testimony which burns in our hearts was not lighted at ancient altars.
Bruce R. McConkie, CR 10/70:127

See also: Latter Days

DIVORCE

Generally, divorce is spelled selfishness on the part of one party, generally both.
Spencer W. Kimball, CR 4/75:7

Many marriages are defeated in the marketplace when unscheduled purchases are made.
Spencer W. Kimball, CR 10/75:6

The remedy for domestic problems and irritations is not divorce, but repentance.
Stephen L Richards, CR 10/54:80

There never could be a divorce in this Church if the husband and wife were keeping the commandments of God.
Stephen L Richards, CR 4/49:136

See also: Marriage

DOVE

The dove is an emblem or token of truth and innocence.
Joseph Smith, HC 5:261

The devil cannot come in the sign of a dove.
Joseph Smith, HC 5:261

See also: Holy Ghost

DREAMS

The Lord has revealed to men by dreams something more than I ever understood or felt before.
Spencer W. Kimball, CR 4/74:173

I claim there never has been anything accomplished
by a man unless he dreamed dreams and had visions
of greater things.
  Levi Edgar Young, CR 4/13:73

See also: Inspiration, Revelation

DUTY

We must not permit fear of criticism to keep us from
doing our duty.
  Ezra Taft Benson, CR 4/73:49

There is no small or unimportant duty in the kingdom
of God.
  Gordon B. Hinckley, CR 10/72:108

There is but one path of safety to the Latter-day
Saints, and that is the path of duty.
  Heber J. Grant, CR 4/15:82

The frailties or failings of others can never be
appropriate reasons for our loss of the blessings we
might have if we ourselves are doing our duty.
  Marion D. Hanks, CR 4/72:128

The greatest and most important duty is to preach the
gospel.
  Joseph Smith, HC 2:478

It is our duty to concentrate all our influence to make
popular that which is sound and good, and unpopular
that which is unsound.
  Joseph Smith, HC 5:286

Our plain duty—so plain that none should
misunderstand it, none can misunderstand it unless
they allow their prejudices and human weaknesses to
prevail over their better judgment; our plain duty is to
live in the spirit of forgiveness, in the spirit of humility
before the Lord, in the love of the truth more than the
love of ourselves and our personal interests.
  Joseph F. Smith, CR 4/09:4

I believe it is your duty, if you see a young boy or girl going wrong, to call the attention of the parent or guardian to it. It may be that you will receive a rebuff, but you will have the satisfaction of having done your duty.
Reed Smoot, CR 10/11:28

Omission of duty leads to commission.
Brigham Young, JD 10:296

EASTER

Easter time is a forceful reminder that the human spirit cannot be confined. It does not deny the reality of death, but it offers us an assurance that God has preserved life beyond the grave.
Franklin D. Richards (1900, 1960-   ), CR 4/75:88

See also: Jesus Christ

EDUCATION

Intelligence is that which enables one to wisely meet the situations of life without education; whereas, education is that which helps one to meet the situations of life without intelligence.
Anon. Stephen L Richards, CR 4/38:23

There is an education that comes through the revelation of the spirit of God to man that is higher than every other class of education, and compared with which all other systems of education sink into insignificance.
Matthias F. Cowley, CR 10/98:9

Learning does not lead to loss of faith. False learning might, but not true learning.
Richard L. Evans, CR 4/56:44

The kingdom of heaven is not for the most learned but for the best.
Charles H. Hart, CR 4/14:116

What each of us needs is a Ph.D. in faith and righteousness.
  Bruce R. McConkie, CR 4/71:99

✳ True education is awakening a love for truth, a just sense of duty, opening the eyes of the soul to the great purpose and end of life.
  David O. McKay, CR 4/65:8

Many an academic giant is at once a spiritual pygmy, and if so, he is usually a moral weakling as well.
  Boyd K. Packer, CR 4/74:138

Education does not change the nature of men; it simply develops and polishes that which is in them; it makes the best of that which there is.
  George Reynolds, JD 26:161

If I were possessed of millions of money I would desire every son of mine to have a trade at his fingers' ends so that if everything were swept away from him he could fall back on his trade and make an honest living.
  Reed Smoot, CR 10/00:7

The foundation of all true education is the wisdom and knowledge of God.
  Erastus Snow, JD 12:178

In relation to the education of the world generally, a great amount of it is of very little value, consisting more of words than ideas.
  John Taylor, JD 5:259

✳The greatest work of the Almighty is to educate his children.
  Rulon S. Wells, CR 4/29:103

Salvation is rather synonymous to the term education.
  Rulon S. Wells, CR 10/31:62

I believe that it is the destiny of this people to become the leaders in education, in knowledge, in understanding and in all those accomplishments

which go to make the perfect man and the perfect
woman.
Rulon S. Wells, CR 4/10:21

See also: Intellect, Knowledge, Teacher, Teaching

EMOTIONS

The springs of human action are inherently in the
feelings, not the intellect.
Joseph B. Wirthlin, CR 4/76:84

Anybody who cannot learn to hear by feeling will not
go very far in the Church.
S. Dilworth Young, CR 10/61:117

See also: Passions

ENDURANCE

The Master who loved most of all, endured the most
and proved his love by his endurance.
Hugh B. Brown, CR 10/54:17

The mark of real conversion is endurance.
Hartman Rector, Jr., CR 4/74:161

If the Saints cannot endure, and endure to the end,
they have no reason to expect eternal salvation.
Brigham Young, JD 3:1

See also: Perseverance

ENEMIES

Those who fight for principle can be proud of the
friends they've gained and the enemies they've earned.
Ezra Taft Benson, CR 4/67:61

The Lord once told me that what I asked for I should
have. I have been afraid to ask God to kill my

enemies, lest some of them should, peradventure, repent.
  Joseph Smith, HC 6:253

I do not want to become so blinded with love for my enemies that I cannot discern between light and darkness, between truth and error, between good and evil.
  Joseph F. Smith, CR 10/07:6

ENVIRONMENT

The most important consideration with reference to children would be the question of environment— environment of the home first, and environment of the Church second.
  Rudger Clawson, CR 10/07:28

We choose carefully the atmosphere that we breathe, that we may live in health. But sometimes, in our carelessness, we place ourselves in subjection to immoral influences that destroy our resistance of evil.
  George Albert Smith, CR 10/29:23

  See also: Nature

EQUALITY

We were not all equal in creation; we are not all equal in authority here; we are not all equal in intelligence. But unless we are one, we are not the Lord's.
  J. Reuben Clark, Jr., CR 4/44:113

Inequality is a law of all social life, and to try to do away with inequality among men is to substitute tyranny for liberty.
  Levi Edgar Young, CR 4/37:114

ERRORS

No matter how many times an error is repeated, it is still an error.
  Richard L. Evans, ACR 8/71:173

I think when we err, we err in that we lose our sense of values or our sense of direction, or do not quite have in mind what will make us happy or unhappy.
  Richard L. Evans, CR 4/59:114

There is no power in error except to destroy.
  George Q. Morris, CR 10/52:69

It does not prove that a man is not a good man because he errs in doctrine.
  Joseph Smith, HC 5:340

ETERNAL LIFE

Religion has to do not only with the internal life of man, but with his eternal life, which will be a continuation of identity and personality into the spiritual realm of immortality.
  Hugh B. Brown, CR 10/62:42

All of us will live forever—somewhere.
  ElRay L. Christiansen, CR 4/58:35

To think of eternal life without eternal love is to construct a paradox.
  Gordon B. Hinckley, CR 4/72:78

The promises of eternal life from God supersede all promises of greatness, comfort, immunities.
  Spencer W. Kimball, ACR 8/72:32

Those who do the Lord's work receive the Lord's wages, even eternal life in his kingdom.
  Bruce R. McConkie, ACR 8/74:90

There is no one great thing that we can do to obtain eternal life.
  David O. McKay, CR 10/14:87

That we should live forever is no greater miracle than that we should live at all.
  Franklin D. Richards (1900, 1960-   ), CR 4/75:88

What price could you pay that would be too high and too great for the blessings of eternal life and to become as your Heavenly Father?

Eldred G. Smith, CR 4/66:42

I do my duty, little by little, day by day, year by year, and then the Lord takes the deeds of my life, and as we use bricks in the building of a house, he builds for me eternal life.

John A. Widtsoe, CR 4/35:81

See also: Eternity

ETERNAL PROGRESSION

The highest reaches of life are but embryonic in the light of eternity, and man has every reason to hope that a future life will afford him full scope for a larger and fuller achievement.

Hugh B. Brown, CR 4/62:107

It is written in the eternity of our God that every soul must progress that does not retrograde.

George Q. Cannon, JD 26:87

There is no such thing as standing still.

Heber J. Grant, CR 4/02:80

God himself, finding he was in the midst of spirits and glory, because he was more intelligent, saw proper to institute laws whereby the rest could have a privilege to advance like himself.

Joseph Smith, HC 6:312

It will be a great work to learn our salvation and exaltation even beyond the grave.

Joseph Smith, HC 6:307

If we are not drawing towards God in principle, we are going from him and drawing towards the Devil.

Joseph Smith, HC 4:588

Man is a dual being, possessed of body and spirit, made in the image of God, and connected with him and with eternity. He is a God in embryo and will live and progress throughout the eternal ages, if obedient to the laws of the Godhead, as the Gods progress throughout the eternal ages.
John Taylor, JD 23:65

See also: Exaltation

ETERNITY

The pleasant future belongs to those who properly use today.
Marvin J. Ashton, CR 4/75:126

Eternity is in process now.
Marvin J. Ashton, CR 4/75:127

We believe in an immortality that has no beginning, just as we believe in an immortality that has no end.
B. H. Roberts, CR 4/04:17

No man can limit the bounds or the eternal existence of eternal time.
Joseph Smith, HC 6:474

We are looked upon by God as though we were in eternity; God dwells in eternity, and does not view things as we do.
Joseph Smith, HC 6:313

I take my ring from my finger and liken it unto the mind of man—the immortal part, because it had no beginning. Suppose you cut it in two; then it has a beginning and end; but join it again, and it continues one eternal round. So with the spirit of man.
Joseph Smith, HC 6:311

The things of man shall endure as man endures, and the things of God are eternal as He is eternal.
James E. Talmage, CR 10/18:59

The present is the outcome of the past; and it is the great hook upon which the future hangs.
Orson F. Whitney, CR 4/16:64

The origin of all things is in eternity.
Brigham Young, JD 7:173

I have been near enough to understand eternity so that I have had to exercise a great deal more faith to desire to live than I ever exercised in my whole life to live.
Brigham Young, JD 14:231

See also: Exaltation, Eternal Progression

EVIL

The evils under which we groan as a people and from which we suffer are not due to any lack of knowledge as to the method or the means that will correct these evils, but they are due to the fact that we ourselves fail to conform to the organization which God has prescribed, which God has revealed.
George Q. Cannon, JD 24:144

We ought to be committed to the principle of not making evil profitable.
Richard L. Evans, CR 4/69:74

It never did make me happy to think of evil, nor to talk about it.
Anthony W. Ivins, CR 4/10:112

Random, individual goodness is not enough in the fight against evil.
Neal A. Maxwell, CR 10/74:15

While virtue, by choice, *will not* associate with filth, evil *cannot* tolerate the presence of light.
Boyd K. Packer, CR 10/73:24

Evils are of two classes; and what are they? First, people do wrong because they do not know how to do

right; second, they do wrong because they are
disposed to do wrong: and do you not see that in
either case they are wrongs?
Charles C. Rich, JD 5:298

See also: Satan, Sin

EVOLUTION

The theory that man is other than the offspring of
God has been, and, so long as it is accepted and acted
upon, will continue to be, a major factor in blocking
man's spiritual growth and in corrupting his morals.
Marion G. Romney, CR 4/73:135

There has been no change in the constitution of man
since he fell.
Joseph Smith, HC 2:17

Any theory that presents as a fact a statement that
man has evolved from other forms, and has not
always been a sentient being, capable of thought, of
reasoning, is in conflict with the word of the Lord.
Joseph Fielding Smith, CR 10/34:64

See also: Science

EXALTATION

[No] one can receive exaltation in the kingdom of our
Heavenly Father at bargain prices.
Joseph Anderson, CR 4/71:96

Beyond our Savior's saving grace no one stands
between us and our own salvation—or exaltation.
Richard L. Evans, CR 4/57:14

Our individual exaltation depends upon our proving
to the Lord that we will at all hazards and under all
circumstances faithfully discharge the trust he has
placed in us.
Marion G. Romney, CR 10/74:103

There are no shortcuts to exaltation.
Robert L. Simpson, CR 4/76:89

Exaltation is salvation added upon; it is an extension
of that idea or condition, just as salvation is an
extension of redemption.
Orson F. Whitney, CR 10/13:97

See also: Eternal Life, Eternal Progression, Eternity,
Immortality, Salvation

EXAMPLE

The most powerful sermon any of us shall ever preach
will be the sermon of our lives.
Melvin J. Ballard, CR 10/34:115

What the teacher is counts for more than what he
says.
Hugh B. Brown, CR 4/63:89

The greatest missionary tool we have is that of
demonstrating friendliness, brotherly kindness,
harmony, love and peace in our homes and in all our
church meetings.
Theodore M. Burton, CR 10/74:77

If parents want their children to be good children they
will have to be good themselves.
Rudger Clawson, CR 10/19:59

It is of very little use to bear testimony that we know
that the Gospel is true unless we exemplify that
testimony in our daily walk and conversation.
Matthias F. Cowley, CR 10/99:62

Example has more followers than reason and is more
forcible than precept.
William J. Critchlow, Jr., CR 10/60:28

A sermon seen is better than a sermon heard.
William J. Critchlow, Jr., CR 10/60:28

The unspoken sermon is heard most clearly and learned most strongly by those near at hand.
Marion D. Hanks, CR 4/74:114

I do not believe we accomplish very much in life unless we are enthusiastic, unless we are in earnest, and unless we practice what we preach.
Heber J. Grant, CR 4/10:40

Among the entire human family, there is no example where the principle of love was demonstrated as perfectly as was shown in the life of Jesus in Palestine.
Milton R. Hunter, CR 10/71:49

Example, example, example in the parents and the older children; therein lies the secret of a successful family.
Harold B. Lee, ACR 8/72:91

In the final analysis, the gospel of God is written, not in the dead letters of the scriptural records, but in the lives of the Saints.
Bruce R. McConkie, CR 10/68:135

When we talk to the world about the need of applying religion, our first duty is to apply it in our lives.
David O. McKay, CR 10/14:89

What you have not defended, your children may reject angrily.
Neal A. Maxwell, CR 10/74:14

The most effective examples a child will ever have—for bad or for good—are his own parents.
H. Burke Peterson, CR 10/72:148

If you make a mistake, all is not lost. You can always be used as a bad example.
Hartman Rector, Jr., CR 10/72:171

The sermon of our own lives will do more to convert the people of the world to the principles of truth, than any other single force or factor that we possess.
Stephen L Richards, CR 4/21:129

We should not claim to be children of God and then go about the world acting as though we are orphans.
Sterling W. Sill, CR 4/70:30

Improper parental example in the home is a leading cause of the wandering of youth from the principles as taught in the gospel of Jesus Christ.
N. Eldon Tanner, CR 10/74:122

EXCOMMUNICATION

No man who today is in full fellowship in the Church, who is receiving the approbation of God, and has the witness of the truth in his heart, who is keeping the commandments of the Lord, who is faithful, pure, virtuous and chaste, will tomorrow be cut off from the Church for adultery, for apostasy, or for wickedness and corruption.
Hyrum M. Smith, CR 4/06:50

There is no place in Zion for the wilful sinner.
Joseph Fielding Smith, CR 4/15:120

See also: Courts

EXPERIENCE

There is no other way by which any man can improve, except by experience.
Heber C. Kimball, JD 9:24

Each time we relive some sacred experience, that experience is renewed in vitality, and we are able to re-absorb the original good.
Sterling W. Sill, CR 4/57:107

EXTREMES

It is necessary sometimes to contemplate things in their extremes, in order that you may beget even a

reasonable amount of activity among the people in any given direction.
B. H. Roberts, CR 4/06:66

There is always danger in extremes.
Hyrum G. Smith, CR 4/21:184

See also: Fanaticism

FAILURE

There is no disgrace in falling down; the disgrace is lying there.
Paul H. Dunn, CR 4/72:107

Any man who tries to do the right thing and continues to try, is not a failure in the sight of God.
J. Golden Kimball, CR 4/07:82

The price of success, freedom, and economic independence is high, but not nearly so high as the price of failure, bankruptcy, heavy indebtedness, and worry.
Thorpe B. Isaacson, CR 4/63:12

It is better to lose than to win an unjust or dishonest cause.
Franklin D. Richards (1900, 1960-   ), CR 10/70:82

The first step toward any failure is always merely to look down, to let earthly things absorb our interests. It is pretty difficult to look down and to look up at the same time.
Sterling W. Sill, CR 4/61:9

Men never fail because of God's revealed word, but rather, in spite of it.
Robert L. Simpson, CR 10/65:77

There is no such word as fail in the lexicon of our Gods.
John Henry Smith, CR 4/00:15

Prosperous times are when the foundation of failures are laid.
Reed Smoot, CR 10/06:39

Man is a manifest failure without the Spirit of God.
George Teasdale, CR 10/00:38

If a man achieves worldly success and does not blend into his life a program of self-improvement to bring about a sensible balance, he no doubt will end up as a failure.
John H. Vandenberg, CR 10/72:26

FAITH

It is not necessary that one see an angel or hear a voice from heaven in order to know that the gospel is true.
Joseph Anderson, ACR 8/73:32

The easiest way to destroy a man's faith is to destroy his morality.
Melvin J. Ballard, CR 4/29:65

Nothing but religious faith has been able to save men from despair.
Hugh B. Brown, CR 10/69:106

Religious faith gives confidence that human tragedy is not a meaningless sport of physical forces.
Hugh B. Brown, CR 10/69:107

Faith is not a substitute for truth, but a pathway to truth.
Hugh B. Brown, CR 10/69:107

The Lord never permits the light of faith wholly to be extinguished in any human heart, however faint the light may glow.
J. Reuben Clark, Jr., CR 10/36:114

Faith is the implementing force of the Priesthood.
J. Reuben Clark, Jr., CR 4/53:54

The principle of faith is as firm as the very pillars of heaven.
Rudger Clawson, CR 10/04:36

The power of faith and the power of God are twin-kindred, godly powers.
William J. Critchlow, Jr., CR 10/65:37

Men today are losing faith in themselves because they have lost faith in God.
Paul H. Dunn, CR 10/67:124

There is nothing wrong with an individual that faith and repentance will not cure.
Alvin R. Dyer, CR 10/69:56

When you find a man of learning who has faith, you may travel with him into new worlds of thought, and beyond horizons as yet not traversed by humankind, with joy and with safety. But when you find a man of learning without faith, you may not travel with him in safety to any destination.
Richard L. Evans, CR 10/39:87

Faith is not rooted in perfect behavior, though it inspires us to desire it, to seek for it.
Marion D. Hanks, CR 4/68:56

Philosophy and theology may be interesting and give us lofty concepts, and we may become inspired by profound thinking, but Christian faith is based upon the simplicity of the gospel, the example, the life, and the teachings of Jesus Christ.
Howard W. Hunter, CR 4/69:138

Faith is the element that builds the bridge in the absence of concrete evidence.
Howard W. Hunter, CR 4/75:57

Those who lack faith live in the past.
Howard W. Hunter, CR 10/62:23

Faith is process.
J. Golden Kimball, CR 4/15:134

If a man profess faith in God and has integrity, he will
adhere to God's commandments.
Anthony W. Ivins, CR 4/16:58

Astronomers have sought knowledge through study,
but prophets through faith.
Spencer W. Kimball, CR 4/62:59

The one who has lost faith has lost more than the
world can give.
Anthon H. Lund, CR 10/15:11

We cannot get faith by logic any more than we can
get learning by simply longing for it.
Richard R. Lyman, CR 4/36:99

A man may say he believes, but if he does nothing to
make that belief or faith a moving power to do, to
accomplish, to produce soul growth, his professing will
avail him nothing.
David O. McKay, CR 4/57:7

To have faith that God is our Father is the safest
anchorage of the soul and brings peace and solace
under any condition.
David O. McKay, CR 10/34:94

Repentance has got to be connected with your faith,
or your faith is good for nothing.
Orson Pratt, JD 7:261

Real faith lets a man *act* as if he knows it is true when
he really doesn't.
Hartman Rector, Jr., CR 10/73:135

Faith, being the moving cause of all action in
temporal as well as spiritual concerns, is evidenced by
an affirmative attitude together with a well-developed
plan of action.
Franklin D. Richards (1900, 1960-   ), CR 4/66:141

If we gave up everything we cannot explain, we would
have to give up life.
  Franklin D. Richards (1900, 1960-   ), CR 4/75:88

Faith comes by investigation.
  George F. Richards, CR 10/14:17

You can't merely snap your fingers and get great faith
in God, any more than you can snap your fingers and
get great musical ability. Faith takes hold of us only
when we take hold of it.
  Sterling W. Sill, CR 4/55:117

A man who has none of the gifts has no faith; and he
deceives himself, if he supposes he has.
  Joseph Smith, HC 5:218

We cannot have faith without belief, but we can
believe without having faith.
  O. Leslie Stone, CR 4/73:90

Eternal vigilance is the price of our faith.
  O. Leslie Stone, CR 4/73:91

Faith is the assurance that God gives us that our
exalted hopes shall be realized.
  Rulon S. Wells, CR 10/31:65

We need not pin our faith to any man's sleeve.
  Daniel H. Wells, JD 16:133

Every doctrine of the Church, every sermon that has
been preached from this pulpit, has to do with faith in
God and repentance from sin.
  Rulon S. Wells, CR 10/33:48

Men cannot have faith in God, nor love him, unless
they are acting in his cause.
  Joseph L. Wirthlin, CR 4/48:147

Faith in the Lord Jesus Christ will give men reason for
their repentance from sin.
  S. Dilworth Young, CR 4/72:84

See also: Belief, Hope, Knowledge, Testimony

FALL

The plan of salvation is as broad as the fall of man.
Reed Smoot, CR 4/33:19

Adam's fall was a step downward, but it was also a step forward.
Orson F. Whitney, CR 4/08:90

See also: Atonement, Jesus Christ

FALSE PROPHETS

False prophets always arise to oppose the true prophets.
Joseph Smith, HC 6:364

The world always mistook false prophets for true ones.
Joseph Smith, HC 4:574

See also: Apostasy

FALSEHOODS

A truth quietly spoken has much greater effect than an untruth shouted from the housetops.
Richard L. Evans, CR 10/38:91

A lie lives only until it is found out, but truth lives and survives.
Heber J. Grant, CR 4/11:22

A lie can travel around the world while truth is getting his boots on.
Heber J. Grant, CR 4/12:28

It is a very difficult thing to undertake to tell a lie and to maintain it.
Heber J. Grant, CR 10/12:49

The very best liars I have any acquaintance with are those who have been cut off from the Church and cast out.
Heber J. Grant, CR 10/31:3

A very simple person can tell the truth, but it takes a very smart person to tell a lie and make it appear like the truth.
Brigham Young, JD 11:304

Truth has, it is quite true, but one enemy, and that is untruth. Untruth has two enemies, truth and itself.
Levi Edgar Young, CR 4/13:73

> *See also:* Truth

FAMILY

The very essence of divine government is fatherhood and the recognition of the family relationship.
Hugh B. Brown, CR 10/66:103

The position of the Church is to aid the parents and the family, not to replace them.
Victor L. Brown, CR 4/72:103

Satan's ultimate goal is to destroy the family, because if he would destroy the family, he will not just have won the battle; he will have won the war.
Victor L. Brown, CR 10/73:137

The family to which we belong is more important than where we live.
Theodore M. Burton, CR 4/75:105

The real measure of success is a man's family.
William J. Critchlow, Jr., CR 10/58:49

Each family in the Church is really a kingdom or government within itself.
James A. Cullimore, CR 10/72:162

Before we create more and more complex social machinery, we ought to put the emphasis back where it belongs, on the oldest social institution in existence—the family, the home.
Richard L. Evans, CR 10/64:135

The praying family is the hope of a better society.
Gordon B. Hinckley, CR 4/63:128

The greatest evil that I know of in this people is the
little bickerings in families.
Orson Hyde, JD 5:283

Nothing on earth would be a greater failure to me
than to fail to keep my family in the Church.
J. Golden Kimball, CR 4/07:82

The family unit is the most important organization in
time or in eternity.
Bruce R. McConkie, CR 4/70:27

The Spirit of God will not strive with a man who in
any way helps to break up another man's family.
David O. McKay, CR 4/69:95

Responsible family membership is a great ideal in the
Church.
Boyd K. Packer, CR 10/74:126

One of the gifts of a loving family is the
encouragement and confidence we receive to magnify
ourselves.
L. Tom Perry, CR 4/73:16

If you spend all your days and save the whole world
but lose your own family, you will be counted as an
unprofitable servant.
Robert L. Simpson, CR 10/73:104

No successful home can be made by the father alone;
no successful home can be made by the mother, alone;
it takes a united family to make a perfect Latter-day
Saint home.
Reed Smoot, CR 10/09:72

Family life changes, not because of any outward
conditions, but because of inner convictions.
A. Theodore Tuttle, CR 10/64:31

In the family relationship, we find our best laboratory in which to practice celestial living.
  A. Theodore Tuttle, CR 10/73:88

  See also: Children, Home, Parents

FAMILY HOME EVENING

The family home evening is an important barrier to works of Satan.
  Ezra Taft Benson, CR 10/71:29

FANATICISM

No man ever accomplished any thing on this earth, without exposing himself by his actions, his earnestness and enthusiasm and zeal, to the charge of fanaticism.
  George Q. Cannon, JD 20:196

  See also: Extremes

FASTING

Observance of the law of the fast is one of the surest ways of preparing ourselves to be spiritually in tune with the Spirit of the Lord.
  Victor L. Brown, ACR 8/71:69

If there were no other virtue in fasting but gaining strength of character, that alone would be sufficient justification for its universal acceptance.
  David O. McKay, CR 4/32:65

A man may fast and pray till he kills himself; and there isn't any necessity for it; nor wisdom in it.
  Joseph F. Smith, CR 10/12:133

The Lord can hear a simple prayer, offered in faith, in half a dozen words, and he will recognize fasting that may not continue more than twenty-four hours, just as

readily and as effectually as he will answer a prayer of a thousand words and fasting for a month.
Joseph F. Smith, CR 10/12:134

There are four factors involved in a proper observance of the fast day, namely; first, abstaining; then, praying; next, testifying; and finally, contributing.
Henry D. Taylor, CR 10/74:19

FATHERHOOD

If fathers are to be respected, they must merit respect; if they are to be loved, they must be consistent, lovable, understanding, and kind, and must honor their priesthood.
Spencer W. Kimball, CR 4/65:63

It should have great meaning that of all the titles of respect and honor and admiration that could be given him, God himself, he who is the highest of all, chose to be addressed simply as Father.
Boyd K. Packer, CR 4/72:139

See also: Family, Man

FAULT-FINDING

I believe in fault-finding for breakfast, dinner and supper, but with our own dear selves.
Heber J. Grant, CR 4/02:60

I want to see you . . . so industrious, so active in the discharge of your duties as Latter-day Saints . . . that you will not have time to spend in magnifying the weaknesses, the follies and the faults of your neighbors and of your fellow members of the Church.
Joseph F. Smith, CR 10/11:10

See also: Criticism, Gossip

FEAR

Fear is the devil's first and chief tool.
John A. Widtsoe, CR 4/50:127

Never serve God because you are afraid of hell; but live your religion, because it is calculated to give you eternal life.
Brigham Young, JD 5:340

FOOD STORAGE

The revelation to store food may be as important to our temporal salvation today as boarding the ark was to the people in the days of Noah.
Ezra Taft Benson, CR 10/73:91

It may be that some time in the future we will survive or starve on what we can produce ourselves.
Marion G. Romney, CR 4/74:179

See also: Preparedness

FORGIVENESS

To the repentant sinner the Church, and we individuals, have all forgiveness; to the repentant sinner we open our arms in welcome; but against the sin which he commits the Church must always war.
J. Reuben Clark, Jr., CR 4/34:95

The ultimate form of love for God and men is forgiveness.
Marion D. Hanks, CR 10/73:15

If we were more liberal in our forgiveness, we would be more encouraging to repentance.
Stephen L Richards, CR 4/56:93

Receiving the Holy Ghost is the therapy which effects forgiveness and heals the sin-sick soul.
Marion G. Romney, CR 4/74:134

Forgiveness is as wide as repentance.
Marion G. Romney, CR 10/55:124

Remittance of sins is the therapy which heals.
Marion G. Romney, CR 10/63:24

As we forgive, we achieve the right to be forgiven.
Robert L. Simpson, CR 10/66:130

No man can find forgiveness for one sin because he is righteous in some other direction.
Hyrum M. Smith, CR 10/17:39

Be ready to forgive our brother on the first intimations of repentance, and asking forgiveness.
Joseph Smith, HC 3:383

God does not look on sin with allowance, but when men have sinned, there must be allowance made for them.
Joseph Smith, HC 5:24

Rather spare ten iniquitous among you, than condemn one innocent one.
Joseph Smith, HC 5:21

Men can be forgiven as long as they have the power to repent.
Orson F. Whitney, CR 4/08:92

An unforgiving spirit is by no means an evidence of strong character; it is quite the reverse.
Abraham O. Woodruff, CR 4/02:32

See also: Repentance

FREE AGENCY

None of us have our free agency to determine the consequences of the choices we make.
William H. Bennett, CR 10/73:85

It was the struggle over free agency that divided us before we came here; it may well be the struggle over

the same principle which will deceive and divide us
again.
Ezra Taft Benson, CR 10/63:16

God never planted his Spirit, his truth, in the hearts of
men from the point of a bayonet.
J. Reuben Clark, Jr., CR 4/57:51

A fundamental principle of the gospel is free agency,
and references in the scriptures show that this
principle is (1) essential to man's salvation; and (2)
may become a measuring rod by which actions of
men, of organizations, of nations may be judged.
David O. McKay, CR 10/65:7

Man's responsibility is correspondingly operative with
his free agency.
David O. McKay, CR 10/65:8

Next to life itself free agency is the greatest gift of God
to man.
David O. McKay, CR 4/52:13

Freedom of choice is more to be treasured than any
possession earth can give.
David O. McKay, CR 4/50:32

Free agency is the impelling force of the soul's
progress.
David O. McKay, CR 4/50:32

Whether born in abject poverty or shackled at birth
by inherited riches, everyone has this most precious of
all life's endowments—the gift of free agency; man's
inherited and inalienable right.
David O. McKay, CR 4/50:32

So fundamental in man's eternal progress is his
inherent right to choose, that the Lord would defend
it even at the price of war.
David O. McKay, CR 4/42:73

There isn't a social order on earth today but what if

we were to follow it long enough and far enough would rob us of our free agency.
Henry D. Moyle, CR 10/47:46

The divine gift agency is not a self-perpetuating endowment.
Marion G. Romney, CR 10/68:65

The preservation of free agency is more important than the preservation of life itself.
Marion G. Romney, CR 10/68:65

The free agency of man is inseparably connected with intelligence.
Erastus Snow, JD 24:158

See also: Agency

FREEDOM

Freedom can be killed by neglect as well as by direct attack.
Ezra Taft Benson, CR 4/73:51

Freedom must be continually won to be enjoyed.
Ezra Taft Benson, CR 10/58:101

When a man stands for freedom, he stands with God.
Ezra Taft Benson, CR 4/67:59

People who are willing . . . to trade freedom for security, are sowing the seeds of destruction and deserve neither freedom nor security.
Ezra Taft Benson, CR 10/54:120

Without the spirit of freedom in the souls of men, there could be no willing response to the gospel plan.
Alvin R. Dyer, CR 4/72:39

We sometimes boast of being in the land of the free, the home of the brave. Nevertheless, we are not free until we have overcome evil—until we liberate ourselves from the bondage of sin.
Rulon S. Wells, CR 4/30:70

See also: Liberty

A friend is a person who will suggest and render the best for us regardless of the immediate consequences.
Marvin J. Ashton, CR 10/72:33

A friend is a possession we earn, not a gift.
Marvin J. Ashton, CR 10/72:33

Whenever a man or woman, young or old, demands as the price of his friendship that you give up the righteous standards of your life, or any of them, that man's friendship is not worth the price he asks.
J. Reuben Clark, Jr., CR 10/38:138

Friendship is not now, and never was, the offspring of debauchery or unrighteousness.
J. Reuben Clark, Jr., CR 10/38:138

If a friend is one who summons us to our best, then is not Jesus Christ our best friend?
David O. McKay, CR 10/29:13

Pure friendship always becomes weakened the very moment you undertake to make it stronger by penal oaths and secrecy.
Joseph Smith, HC 3:303

Friendship is one of the grand fundamental principles of "Mormonism."
Joseph Smith, HC 5:517

I have never lost a friend that was worthy of being a friend, from living as near as I could to the requirements of the gospel.
Reed Smoot, CR 10/16:39

A man is no friend to himself if he rejects the laws of God. He is unkind to himself when he ignores principles that lead to everlasting life.
George Teasdale, CR 10/03:51

If the Lord has any friends on earth they are the Saints of God, and if the Saints of God have any

friends anywhere, they consist of the God of Israel and the heavenly hosts, and the spirits of just men made perfect.
Wilford Woodruff, CR 4/80:7

GATHERING

Every nation is the gathering place for its own people.
Bruce R. McConkie, ACR 8/72:45

GENEALOGY

The key to true spirituality is priesthood genealogy.
Theodore M. Burton, CR 10/66:35

Shall we not be interested in every soul that has passed away? Must not the chain be made complete and the dead be connected with the living, and the living with the dead? Otherwise, we shall be rejected as a church.
Rudger Clawson, CR 10/00:10

If we refuse to recognize our obligation to do the work for our dead the Lord will reject us as a church.
Rudger Clawson, CR 10/40:123

We work for those who live and also for the dead, thus following in the footsteps of our Lord and Master.
Francis M. Lyman, CR 4/11:15

There are churches whose members believe in praying for the dead; but we believe in working for the dead.
Anthon H. Lund, CR 10/03:80

Of all Christian service vicarious work for the dead is the most Christ-like.
Stephen L Richards, CR 4/38:25

If the whole Church should go to with all their might to save their dead, seal their posterity, and gather their living friends, and spend none of their time in behalf of the world, they would hardly get through

before night would come, when no man can work.
Joseph Smith, HC 6:184

The greatest responsibility in this world that God has laid upon us is to seek after our dead.
Joseph Smith, HC 6:313

See also: Temple

GENERAL AUTHORITIES (See Leadership)

GOD

Our Father in Heaven is not an umpire who is trying to count us out. He is not a competitor who is trying to outsmart us. He is not a prosecutor who is trying to convict us. He is a loving father who wants our happiness and eternal progress and everlasting opportunity and glorious accomplishment.
Richard L. Evans, ACR 8/71:64

Remember that God, our Heavenly Father, was perhaps once a child, and mortal like we ourselves, and rose step by step by step in the scale of progress, in the school of advancement; has moved forward and overcome, until he has arrived at the point where he now is.
Orson Hyde, JD 1:123

Unless we are willing to prepare for a new dark age, we must soon acknowledge that as good as we think we are, we are not good enough to get along without the God our forefathers found indispensable.
Thorpe B. Isaacson, CR 4/58:103

If we are to know God, we must believe as he believes, think as he thinks, and experience what he experiences.
Bruce R. McConkie, CR 4/72:134

God is not viewed from the standpoint of what we may get from him, but what we may give to him.
David O. McKay, CR 10/53:10

The greatest comfort that can come to us in this life is
to sense the realization of communion with God.
  David O. McKay, CR 4/46:114

If the inhabitants of all the worlds of the universe were
scribes, every blade of grass a pen, and every ocean
ink, they could not write all the doings of the
Almighty, of His servants, and of His angels.
  Parley P. Pratt, JD 1:307-8

The field of God's activity is not confined to his
Church and inspiration from him is not limited to the
general authorities of the Church or its membership.
  George F. Richards, CR 10/19:63

There is nothing other than a knowledge of the living
and true God which will give men incentives strong
enough to induce them to root out of their lives the
wickedness which has brought us to the brink of the
cataclysm on which we totter.
  Marion G. Romney, CR 10/64:51

In fighting against God we are sinning against
ourselves.
  Sterling W. Sill, CR 10/64:111

God has not gone out of business.
  Sterling W. Sill, CR 4/63:43

The great majority of mankind do not comprehend
anything, either that which is past, or that which is to
come, as it respects their relationship to God.
  Joseph Smith, HC 6:303

God himself is a self-existing being. . . . Man exists
upon the same principles.
  Joseph Smith, HC 6:310

It is the first principle of the gospel to know for a
certainty the character of God.
  Joseph Smith, HC 6:305

You cannot go anywhere but where God can find you.
  Joseph Smith, HC 6:366

It is no more incredible that God should *save* the dead, than that he should *raise* the dead.
  Joseph Smith, HC 4:425

In knowledge there is power. God has more power than all other beings, because he has greater knowledge; and hence he knows how to subject all other beings to him. He has power over all.
  Joseph Smith, HC 5:340

The great Parent of the universe looks upon the whole of the human family with a fatherly care and paternal regard.
  Joseph Smith, HC 4:595

God himself was once as we are now, and is an exalted man, and sits enthroned in yonder heavens! That is the great secret.
  Joseph Smith, HC 6:305

The mind or the intelligence which man possesses is co-equal with God himself.
  Joseph Smith, HC 6:310

If there was anything great or good in the world, it came from God.
  Joseph Smith, HC 5:63

We admit that God is the great source and fountain from whence proceeds all good; that He is perfect intelligence and that His wisdom is alone sufficient to govern and regulate the mighty creations and worlds which shine and blaze with such magnificence and splendor over our heads, as though touched with His finger and moved by His Almighty word.
  Joseph Smith, HC 2:12

Our heavenly Father is more liberal in His views, and boundless in His mercies and blessings, than we are ready to believe or receive; and, at the same time, is more terrible to the workers of iniquity, more awful in the executions of His punishments, and more ready to

detect every false way, than we are apt to suppose
Him to be.
  Joseph Smith, HC 5:136

The grandest conception of "Mormonism" is our
conception of God.
  John A. Widtsoe, CR 10/21:48

The great need of the world today is a correct
understanding of God.
  John A. Widtsoe, CR 10/21:49

The only path to peace and happiness is through the
proper knowledge of God.
  John A. Widtsoe, CR 10/21:49

GODHOOD

You have got to learn how to be Gods yourselves, and
to be kings and priests to God, the same as all gods
have done before you, namely, by going from one
small degree to another, and from a small capacity to
a great one.
  Joseph Smith, HC 6:306

  See also: Man

GOLDEN RULE

The measure of peace that we have or shall have will
be proportionate to the degree of fulness to which the
aggressor observes the Golden Rule.
  Joseph F. Merrill, CR 4/50:58

The Golden Rule, made up of 17 words is probably
the greatest formula for any business success that has
ever been known in the world.
  Sterling W. Sill, CR 10/68:137

  See also: Love

GOODNESS

Look for the good; build up the good; sustain the good; and speak as little about the evil as you possibly can.
Joseph F. Smith, CR 4/13:8

As long as you are good you will be great. But, if you cease to be good you will cease to be great.
Henry D. Taylor, ACR 8/71:149

The three great characteristics of creation are truth, beauty, and goodness.
Levi Edgar Young, CR 4/44:38

GOSPEL

The ark was the means of salvation to those former days, it shall be the gospel of the Lord Jesus Christ in these latter-days.
Melvin J. Ballard, CR 4/25:133-34

The restored gospel can only thrive in an atmosphere of liberty.
Ezra Taft Benson, CR 10/62:17

For the righteous the gospel provides a warning before a calamity, a program for the crises, a refuge for every disaster.
Ezra Taft Benson, CR 10/73:90

The teachings of the Gospel are the very essence of social justice.
Sylvester Q. Cannon, CR 10/33:32

The gospel of Jesus Christ claims our obedience, whether we receive the gifts of the Spirit or not.
George Q. Cannon, JD 11:332

The gospel . . . is the Great Physician's unfailing prescription for troubled souls.
William J. Critchlow, Jr., CR 4/64:32

The gospel of Jesus Christ will not flower or expand its influence under conditions where the will of the individual is suppressed.
Alvin R. Dyer, CR 4/72:39

I cannot say how good I am, but I know that without the gospel I would be less good.
Alvin R. Dyer, CR 4/67:109-10

I know that the gospel tree is alive, that fruit grows upon the tree, as I have reached out my hand and plucked the fruit thereof, and have eaten it.
Heber J. Grant, CR 4/01:64

The gospel is not a philosophy of repression, as so many regard it. It is a plan of freedom that gives discipline to appetite and direction to behavior.
Gordon B. Hinckley, CR 4/65:78

We need no security other than the gospel.
Thorpe B. Isaacson, CR 4/53:91

As we incline our hearts to our Heavenly Father and his son Jesus Christ, we hear a symphony of sweet music sung by heavenly voices proclaiming the gospel of peace.
Spencer W. Kimball, CR 4/74:65

The teachings of the gospel of Jesus Christ are drills in the battle of life, but if we fail to keep the commandments of God, we lose the battle.
Harold B. Lee, ACR 8/72:48

The gospel finds its greatest expression in the individual.
David O. McKay, CR 10/67:149

The mission of the gospel of Jesus Christ [is]—to make evil-minded men and women good, and to make good men and women better: in other words, to change men's lives, to change human nature.
David O. McKay, CR 10/58:94

The restored gospel is a rational philosophy that teaches men how to get happiness in this life and exaltation in the life to come.
David O. McKay, CR 4/59:74

The gospel is not merely a gospel for one age, for one people, for one place—it is a gospel for the galaxies!
Neal A. Maxwell, CR 4/75:150

One protective principle of the gospel is better than a thousand compensatory governmental programs—which programs are, so often, like "straightening deck chairs on the Titanic."
Neal A. Maxwell, CR 10/74:15

Only the gospel can really help us avoid the painful excess in the tug-of-war between the need for liberty and the need for order.
Neal A. Maxwell, CR 4/75:150

The gospel might be likened to the keyboard of a piano—a full keyboard with a selection of keys on which one who is trained can play a variety without limits; a ballad to express love, a march to rally, a melody to soothe, and a hymn to inspire; an endless variety to suit every mood and satisfy every need.
Boyd K. Packer, CR 10/71:9

The gospel stands as true for those who reject it as for those who accept it—both will be judged by it.
Boyd K. Packer, CR 10/74:127

When men go outside of the church of Jesus Christ for anything that they believe will benefit them, it shows that they have a narrow, a limited and a contracted idea of the Gospel, and do not rightly understand its principles nor its efficacy for salvation day by day and forever.
George Reynolds, CR 4/06:25

The gospel . . . is God's own guide to a perfect life.
George F. Richards, CR 10/06:67

This gospel we have received is one of sacrifice, service and self-abnegation from beginning to end. That is what constitutes the straight and narrow way that leads to life eternal.
George F. Richards, CR 10/20:39

The gospel is broad enough, and deep enough, and of such towering heights as to surpass the powers of the greatest mind to comprehend, and yet so simple in its fundamentals as to satisfy the honest inquiry of the child.
Stephen L Richards, CR 4/18:163

The gospel fulfills every requirement of a human life.
Stephen L Richards, CR 4/20:99

This gospel has often been spoken of as a way of life. This however is not quite accurate. Consisting as it does of the principles and ordinances necessary to man's exaltation, it is not just *a* way of life, it is *the* one and only way of life by which men may accomplish the full purpose of their mortality.
Marion G. Romney, CR 10/58:95

The Gospel of Jesus Christ is a gospel of blessing, not a gospel of boasting, not a gospel of faultfinding and criticism, but a gospel of industry, purity, obedience, peace, love, charity, kindness, faith and patience.
George Albert Smith, CR 4/35:44

There is no cure for the ills of the world except the gospel of the Lord Jesus Christ.
Joseph Fielding Smith, CR 4/72:13

The Gospel of Jesus Christ is the perfect law of liberty.
Joseph F. Smith, JD 12:330

More is included in the gospel than all Scripture thus far written.
James E. Talmage, CR 4/18:160

No teaching of the gospel restricts us in any way in anything that is worthwhile.
N. Eldon Tanner, ACR 8/72:10

There are two vital principles in the everlasting gospel; one is faith and the other is love.
George Teasdale, CR 10/06:31

What the light of the sun is to the flower, causing it to unfold from within and turn to the source of light, so the gospel light is to the soul of man.
A. Theodore Tuttle, CR 10/64:31

The Gospel of the Lord Jesus Christ is a panacea for every affliction of the soul of man.
Rulon S. Wells, CR 4/14:112

We have no right to take the theories of men, however, scholarly, however learned and set them up as a standard, and try to make the Gospel bow down to them; making of them an iron bedstead upon which God's truth if not long enough, must be stretched out, or if too long, must be chopped off—anything to make it fit into the system of men's thoughts and theories! On the contrary, we should hold up the Gospel as the standard of truth, and measure thereby the theories and opinions of men.
Orson F. Whitney, CR 4/15:100

The gospel is the plan of eternal progression, and perfection is its goal.
Orson F. Whitney, CR 10/20:36

Every question confronting humanity may be answered by the gospel.
John A. Widtsoe, CR 4/45:92

The Gospel of Christ is not a mere life boat or fire escape—a way out of a perilous situation. It is all this and more. It is the path to endless glory and exaltation, the plan of eternal progression.
Orson F. Whitney, CR 10/25:101

There is a gnawing hunger in the human heart that, if not fed by the truths of the gospel, leaves life empty and devoid of peace.
Joseph B. Wirthlin, CR 10/75:154

What the sun in the heavenly blue is to the earth
struggling to get free from winter's grip, so the gospel
is to sorrowing souls yearning for something higher
and better than mankind has yet found.
Joseph L. Wirthlin, CR 10/47:121

The gospel will revolutionize the whole world of
mankind.
Brigham Young, JD 12:113

The Gospel of life and salvation is a Gospel of
repentance.
Seymour B. Young, CR 4/98:74

See also: Church, Gospel Plan, Mormonism

GOSPEL PLAN

The way of the Lord can eliminate wars, riots,
discrimination, suffering, and starvation.
Theodore M. Burton, CR 10/71:74

The finite mind is not capable of wholly
comprehending the great plan of redemption.
Rudger Clawson, CR 10/04:35

No matter how near the world come to the theories of
the Gospel, no matter how much they try to establish
them, without the Spirit of the Gospel and the
authority of the Holy Priesthood they never can carry
them out, worlds without end.
Matthias F. Cowley, CR 10/03:52

God has established His work, and within it is found
every element that is essential for the salvation of the
people, temporally and spiritually.
Matthias F. Cowley, CR 10/03:53

Without the spirit of freedom in the souls of men,
there could be no willing response to the gospel plan.
Alvin R. Dyer, CR 4/72:39

God has written the score which we are to perform. Our prophet is our director. With effort and with harmony we can stir the world and "crown him Lord of all," if we have the will to discipline ourselves with that restraint which comes of true testimony.
    Gordon B. Hinckley, CR 10/61:116

Our mission is two-fold, to save all the living who will believe, and to warn all who reject the truth; that they may be left without excuse and to redeem the dead from their sins, or at least put the means within their hands, which were denied them in this life and of which they can partake in the spirit, that they also might receive salvation as well as we.
    Joseph Fielding Smith, CR 4/12:68

Those who will receive diplomas in the school of God must take the course outlined in its curriculum which provides that men shall not only know the truth, but also do it.
    Rulon S. Wells, CR 10/22:120

God's work is progressive. It changes its appearance, but never its principles.
    Orson F. Whitney, CR 10/16:56

You cannot find a compass on the earth, that points, so directly, as the Gospel plan of salvation. It has a place for everything, and puts everything in its place. It divides, and sub-divides, and gives to every portion of the human family, as circumstances require.
    Brigham Young, JD 3:96

    See also: Baptism, Faith, Holy Ghost, Repentance

GOSSIP

Gossip bespeaks either a vacant mind or one that entertains jealousy or envy.
    David O. McKay, CR 10/54:132

Gossip brings discord and thrives best in superficial

minds, as fungi grows best on weakened plants.
David O. McKay, CR 10/38:134

Gossip is the worst form of judging.
N. Eldon Tanner, CR 4/72:57

See also: Fault-Finding

GOVERNMENT

No nation can fully preserve its institutions and
wholly disregard God.
Melvin J. Ballard, CR 10/29:50

Every organization and institution that promotes the
welfare of one particular class against the welfare and
interest of others, is dangerous.
Melvin J. Ballard, CR 4/22:85

Man is superior to government and should remain
master over it.
Ezra Taft Benson, CR 10/68:18

The smaller the governmental unit and the closer it is
to the people, the easier it is to guide it, to correct it, to
keep it solvent, and to keep our freedom.
Ezra Taft Benson, CR 10/68:19

If we accept the premise that human rights are
granted by government, then we must be willing to
accept the corollary that they can be denied by
government.
Ezra Taft Benson, CR 10/68:18

Great nations are never conquered from outside unless
they are rotten inside.
Ezra Taft Benson, CR 4/68:50

There is great safety in a nation on its knees.
Ezra Taft Benson, CR 4/73:53

Unless the people bake one loaf of bread for each

citizen, the government cannot guarantee that each will have one loaf to eat.
Ezra Taft Benson, CR 10/68:20

Ships and tanks and airplanes and guns, while necessary implements for waging physical warfare are not the real source of a nation's strength. Its strength lies in the basic integrity of its people and that depends upon the beliefs they cherish which fashion their lives.
Albert E. Bowen, CR 10/45:68

Good government can be had only if administered by *good men,* selected by *good citizens.*
ElRay L. Christiansen, CR 10/67:139

Without God's aid, we shall not preserve our political heritage neither to our own blessing, nor to the blessing of our posterity, nor to the blessing of the down-trodden peoples of the world.
J. Reuben Clark, Jr., CR 4/57:52

There is no strength comparable to the strength of a nation whose people know the meaning of sacrifice.
Thorpe B. Isaacson, CR 4/59:64

Every Latter-day Saint should sustain, honor and obey the constitutional law of the land in which he lives.
Spencer W. Kimball, CR 4/74:5

No nation will become great whose trusted officers will pass legislation for personal gain, who will take advantage of public office for personal preferment, or to gratify vain ambition, or who will, through forgery, chicanery, and fraud, rob the government, or be false in office to a public trust.
David O. McKay, CR 4/64:6

A clean man is a national asset. A pure woman is the incarnation of true national glory.
David O. McKay, CR 4/65:8

The government is best which has as its aim the administration of justice, social well-being and the promotion of prosperity among its members.
David O. McKay, CR 4/30:80

No nation is greater than its spiritual concepts.
Alma Sonne, CR 10/42:19

See also: Citizenship, Nationalism, Patriotism, Politics

GRATITUDE

✓Gratitude is the memory of the heart.
Paul H. Dunn, CR 10/70:14

Absence of gratitude is the mark of the narrow, uneducated mind. It bespeaks a lack of knowledge and the ignorance of self-sufficiency. It expresses itself in ugly egotism and frequently in wanton mischief.
Gordon B. Hinckley, CR 10/64:117

Thankfulness is measured by the number of words; gratitude is measured by the nature of our actions.
David O. McKay, CR 10/55:4

I have never seen a happy person who was not thankful.
Hartman Rector, Jr., CR 4/73:86

The kindness of a man should never be forgotten.
Joseph Smith, HC 1:444

✓The spirit of gratitude always brings happiness.
John Wells, CR 4/35:125

GREATNESS

The only measure of true greatness is how close a man can become like Jesus.
Ezra Taft Benson, CR 10/72:53

Virtue lies at the foundation of greatness.
George Q. Cannon, JD 24:225

Permissiveness never produced greatness.
Gordon B. Hinckley, CR 4/73:73

When people stand for principle, and know by their faith in God that the principle is true, it is always a mark of true greatness.
Levi Edgar Young, CR 4/19:29

See also: Success

HABITS

If you can control your thoughts, you can overcome habits.
Boyd K. Packer, CR 10/73:24

We pick up our worst habits from our best friends.
H. Burke Peterson, ACR 8/73:62

The diminutive chains of habit are generally too small to be felt until they are too strong to be broken.
Franklin D. Richards (1900, 1960-   ), CR 10/70:80

It is just as easy to form good habits as it is to form evil ones.
Joseph Fielding Smith, CR 4/68:11

See also: Sin

HAPPINESS

There are two ways to be happy. One is to increase your income and the other is to diminish your expenses.
Anon. Sylvester Q. Cannon, CR 10/29:46

The truly happy people are those who have faith in the Lord and keep the laws of the gospel, those who forget self in their desire and effort to bless others.
Joseph Anderson, CR 4/75:44

Happiness is a by-product of service.
William J. Critchlow, Jr., CR 10/58:51

If we shall miss realizing our highest happiness and possibilities and opportunities and progress and peace and development, it will not be because of what we do not know, it will be because of what we ignore.
  Richard L. Evans, CR 10/52:126

Happiness comes from within, and not from without.
  Milton R. Hunter, CR 4/54:129

The measure of a people's happiness comes in proportion to the amount of love they have in their hearts for their fellowmen.
  Milton R. Hunter, CR 10/66:39

You never saw a man in your life do a wrong thing, who was happy over it.
  J. Golden Kimball, CR 4/08:117

The man who is ambitious for personal gain and personal advantage is never a hap˖˙y man, for before him always are the receding horizons of life that will ever mock his attempts at acquisition and conquest. That man who serves unselfishly is the man who is the happy man.
  Harold B. Lee, CR 4/47:49-50

Man's greatest happiness comes from losing himself for the good of others.
  David O. McKay, CR 10/63:8

There is no happiness without peace.
  David O. McKay, CR 10/53:132

There are seeds of happiness planted in every human soul. Our mental attitude and disposition constitute the environment in which these seeds may germinate.
  David O. McKay, CR 10/34:92

If you want to be miserable, just harbor hate for a brother, and if you want to hate, just do your brother some injury. But if you would be happy, render a kind service, make somebody else happy.
  David O. McKay, CR 10/36:104-5

89

Happiness is not an external condition, it is a state of the spirit and attitude of the mind.
David O. McKay, CR 10/34:93

I have never seen a happy person who was not thankful.
Hartman Rector, Jr., CR 4/73:86

Happiness in the life of the Latter-day Saint consists in the consciousness of having lived closely to the law of the Lord.
George F. Richards, CR 10/14:17

I have never seen happier people than those who have repented.
Stephen L Richards, CR 10/40:35

The key to happiness is to get the spirit and keep it.
Marion G. Romney, CR 10/61:61

The finest recipe that I could give, to obtain happiness, would be: Keep the commandments of the Lord.
George Albert Smith, CR 10/34:47-48

Our eternal happiness will be in proportion to the way that we devote ourselves to helping others.
George Albert Smith, CR 10/36:71

Happiness is the object and design of our existence; and will be the end thereof, if we pursue the path that leads to it; and this path is virtue, uprightness, faithfulness, holiness and keeping all the commandments of God.
Joseph Smith, HC 5:134-35

Without unity and confidence no faithful Latter-day Saint can be truly happy.
Joseph F. Smith, JD 25:51

Men are not created to be miserable.
N. Eldon Tanner, CR 4/73:60

There is no real happiness in having or getting, but only in giving.
N. Eldon Tanner, CR 4/67:104

There is no true happiness except that which comes from a faithful performance of duty, under the gift and power of the Holy Ghost.
John W. Taylor, CR 10/03:40

There is no happiness in this world that is superior to the happiness of the man or woman that loves God and keeps His commandments.
George Teasdale, CR 10/98:40

The happiest people on earth are those who contribute to the welfare of their neighbors and friends.
John Wells, CR 10/34:31

If we take eternal truth as the woof of the pattern, and human experience as the warp, just as we make a pattern of linen or of cotton, . . . then we shall weave into it that thing which we call human happiness.
John A. Widtsoe, CR 4/31:61

Wealth never was the source of happiness to any person. It cannot be: it is not in the nature of things; for contentment exists only in the mind. In the mind there is happiness—in the mind there is glory.
Brigham Young, JD 7:159

See also: Joy, Peace

HEAVEN

Pure hearts in a pure home are always in whispering distance of heaven.
Anon. David O. McKay, CR 4/64:5

The only road to heaven is the road of service.
Charles A. Callis, CR 4/39:126

Heaven is a place, but also a condition.
  Spencer W. Kimball, CR 10/71:156

I picture heaven as a continuation of the ideal home.
  David O. McKay, CR 4/64:5

Make home your hobby, for, if anyone makes a loving
home with all his heart, he can never miss heaven.
  Anon. David O. McKay, CR 4/35:116

To think that God cares for nothing but singing and
praying, and that some time we will sit on the corner
of a cloud twanging a harp through all eternity, and
that is to be our heaven, is an absurdity to my mind.
  Charles W. Penrose, CR 4/05:72

The powers on high are with the powers on the earth.
  Charles W. Penrose, CR 4/19:34

The heaven we seek is little more than the projection
of our homes into eternity.
  Stephen L Richards, CR 4/47:90

One can get to heaven on half the effort that we
usually burn up in going to hell.
  Sterling W. Sill, CR 10/62:38

If we want to be great souls in heaven, we should
practice being great souls here.
  Sterling W. Sill, CR 10/62:39

Could you gaze into heaven five minutes, you would
know more than you would by reading all that ever
was written on the subject.
  Joseph Smith, HC 6:50

HELL

It matters not how beautiful a place it may be,—
although it is as lovely as the garden of Eden—though
everything in the eternal world harmonizes and the
elements all conspire to produce happiness, yet place a

people there with wicked hearts and it is hell.
Orson Pratt, JD 7:89

If we should find a better people before ourselves are grown better, we could not live among them, and that would be the hell of it.
Parley P. Pratt, JD 1:87

To hell there is an exit as well as an entrance.
James E. Talmage, CR 4/30:97

Hell is not paved with good intentions; it would be more appropriate to say it is paved with evil intentions.
Rulon S. Wells, CR 4/10:22

See also: Spiritual Death

HEREDITY

One thing we often fail to realize is that our priesthood comes to us through the lineage of our fathers and mothers.
Theodore M. Burton, CR 4/75:103

Knowledge pertaining to the gospel of Jesus Christ does not come through ordination, nor by appointment, nor by lineage, nor through father and mother, though they are helpful.
J. Golden Kimball, CR 4/13:85

The only true aristocracy in the world is the aristrocracy of righteousness, and the only families that will persist are those who keep the commandments of our Heavenly Father.
George Albert Smith, CR 4/46:125

See also: Family

HEROES

The greatest hero, if you will, who has ever lived is the

Savior of mankind, Jesus Christ.
  Victor L. Brown, CR 10/70:124

There is no life of the mind or aspiration of the spirit without emulation of great heroes.
  Levi Edgar Young, CR 10/58:64

HOLY GHOST

When we have the Spirit of truth dwelling in our hearts, we are ready, and not only ready but willing to do the things that are required at our hands.
  Ezra T. Benson, JD 6:261

The Spirit of God will not dwell in a man that has evil desires and does not try to quench them.
  George Q. Cannon, CR 10/97:68

Though a man may be very learned in the ancient and modern sciences, may have travelled extensively, may understand the various phases of human nature, and be thoroughly acquainted with the history of our race so far as it has been handed down to us, yet, if he have not the Spirit of God, his knowledge fades away if placed alongside that of the otherwise ignorant Saint, for it is found insufficient to reveal to him that this is the work of God.
  George Q. Cannon, JD 11:333

There are so many subjects that are intimately connected with our lives and with the growth and development of the work, that a man cannot be at a loss for something to say, if he has the Spirit of the Lord.
  George Q. Cannon, CR 4/99:63

When the Holy Ghost is really within us, Satan must remain without.
  ElRay L. Christiansen, CR 10/74:30

Man can serve man by the spirit of man, but in order to be a servant of God we must have the spirit of God.
  Rudger Clawson, CR 10/99:3

When I became excited, fanatical, and over-zealous, I mistakenly thought it was the Spirit of the Lord, but have learned better, as the Holy Ghost does not operate that way.
  J. Golden Kimball, CR 4/07:81

The Latter-day Saints are as sensitive to the movements and operations of the Spirit of the Lord as the thermometer is to the presence of heat and cold.
  Francis M. Lyman, CR 4/01:48-49

The Holy Ghost in the hearts of the Elders of Israel makes them the living oracles of God, and they are entitled to speak by the inspiration of the Holy Ghost.
  Francis M. Lyman, CR 10/97:18

What the sunshine is to the field and to the flowers the Holy Spirit is to the life of man.
  David O. McKay, CR 10/30:10

If we live worthy of divine guidance, as we are privileged to do, we shall not go very far astray.
  Joseph F. Merrill, CR 10/40:77

This work will always be distinguished from the works of men, in that there will be imminent in it the Spirit of God working His sovereign will.
  B. H. Roberts, CR 10/03:78

The hallmark of the church of Christ, distinguishing it from all other churches and forms of worship, has ever been the receiving of the gift of the Holy Ghost by the membership of the Church.
  Marion G. Romney, CR 4/74:134

Without [the gift of the Holy Ghost] the Church would be as dead and impotent as an electric powerhouse without electricity.
  Marion G. Romney, CR 10/72:77

No person whose soul is illuminated by the burning Spirit of God can in this world of sin and dense darkness remain passive.
  Marion G. Romney, CR 10/41:89

The . . . Holy Ghost has no other effect than pure intelligence.
Joseph Smith, HC 3:380

Nothing is a greater injury to the children of men that to be under the influence of a false spirit when they think they have the Spirit of God.
Joseph Smith, HC 4:573

No man can receive the Holy Ghost without receiving revelations.
Joseph Smith, HC 6:58

The sun shines upon the evil and the good; but the Holy Ghost descends only upon the righteous and upon those that are forgiven of their sins.
Joseph F. Smith, JD 24:176

If we falter and turn aside, our lamp will burn dim and finally go out, when lo, the Comforter, the source of revelation, will leave us, and darkness will take its place; then how great will be that darkness!
Joseph F. Smith, JD 18:273

It is vain for the Lord to communicate his will unto the people unless the people possess a portion of his Spirit, to comprehend something of that will and the designs of God towards them.
John Taylor, JD 11:158

Man is a manifest failure without the Spirit of God.
George Teasdale, CR 10/00:38

Faith in God is a prerequisite to the influence of the Holy Spirit.
John H. Vandenberg, CR 10/71:140

The things of God should be surveyed by the light of the Spirit of God, not by the flickering candle of human wisdom.
Orson F. Whitney, CR 4/31:64

The Spirit of the Lord is the food of our spirits.
Orson F. Whitney, CR 4/31:62

Unless you have the Holy Ghost with you when you go out to preach the gospel, you cannot do your duty.
Wilford Woodruff, CR 4/98:32

Were your faith concentrated upon the proper object, your confidence unshaken, your lives pure and holy, every one fulfilling the duties of his or her calling according to the Priesthood and capacity bestowed upon you, you would be filled with the Holy Ghost, and it would be as impossible for any man to deceive and lead you to destruction as for a feather to remain unconsumed in the midst of intense heat.
Brigham Young, JD 7:277

When you see a person endowed by the Holy Ghost, you need not expect him to look and act precisely as you do.
Brigham Young, JD 9:122

See also: Inspiration, Spiritual, Spirituality, Revelation

HOME

There can be no genuine happiness separate and apart from the home.
Ezra Taft Benson, CR 10/47:27

The real man is seen and known in the comparative solitude of the home.
Hugh B. Brown, CR 4/62:88

This world will be no better than its homes.
Richard L. Evans, ACR 8/71:71

There never was a tonic that would cure more social ailments than a healthy, happy home.
Richard L. Evans, CR 10/64:135

Home life, home teaching, parental guidance is the panacea for all the ailments, a cure for all diseases, a remedy for all problems.
Spencer W. Kimball, CR 4/65:65

The greatest of the Lord's work you brethren will ever do as fathers will be within the walls of your own home.
Harold B. Lee, CR 4/73:130

Neither school nor the world can reform the finished product of a bad home.
Harold B. Lee, CR 4/65:13

We are measured best with respect to our religion in our own homes.
Richard R. Lyman, CR 10/20:154-55

The most vicious enemy to home life is immorality.
David O. McKay, CR 10/69:7

No other success can compensate for failure in the home.
David O. McKay, CR 4/64:5

Let calmness be characteristic of our home life.
David O. McKay, CR 4/59:75

Take your sons with you along this road of life, that you may have them with you in that eternal home where there is everlasting peace and contentment.
David O. McKay, CR 10/09:89

The united, well-ordered American home is one of the greatest contributing factors to the preservation of the Constitution of the United States.
David O. McKay, CR 4/35:110

Would you have a strong and virile nation, keep your homes pure—would you reduce deliquency and crime, lessen the number of broken homes.
David O. McKay, CR 4/35:115

The home is the incubator either of children of high character or of criminals.
David O. McKay, CR 4/35:115

In the well-ordered home we may experience a taste of

heaven.
David O. McKay, CR 4/43:19

Make home your hobby, for, if anyone makes a loving home with all his heart, he can never miss heaven.
Anon. David O. McKay, CR 4/35:116

Our measure will not depend on academic degrees or political preference or property or influence so much as simply how we live at home.
Boyd K. Packer, CR 10/63:64

The gospel of Jesus Christ is easier taught and longer remembered in a happy home.
H. Burke Peterson, ACR 8/73:63

The home is the nursery not only of all human beings but of all virtue.
Stephen L Richards, CR 10/41:105

There ought to be a difference between homes presided over by the power of the priesthood and those homes which are not.
Stephen L Richards, CR 4/26:82

Termites are permeating the foundation of the kingdom—the homes of the people—even more destructive and elusive than those semi-microscopic little animals that break down our walls. Corrective measures are imperative.
Stephen L Richards, CR 4/58:93-94

The strength of a nation is the home; the basis of the Church is the home; anything that interferes with the desire and love of home affects the nation and the Church.
Reed Smoot, CR 10/10:70

The home is the teaching unit of the Church.
A. Theodore Tuttle, CR 10/69:131

When each man sets his own house in order, the whole world will be in order.
John A. Widtsoe, CR 10/36:98

The home is the only eternal organization.
S. Dilworth Young, CR 10/69:40

See also: Family, Parents

HOME TEACHING

Home teaching is never done.
James A. Cullimore, CR 10/72:165

No effort to redeem your youth can be more productive than the time and attention given to priesthood home teaching.
Boyd K. Packer, CR 10/72:102

HONESTY

A man may be a very honest man financially, and yet not be honest enough to receive the truth of heaven.
George Q. Cannon, CR 4/98:7

To be honest means that we are in harmony with divine law.
David O. McKay, CR 10/08:108

Loyalty is akin to honesty; and if you are not honest, you are really not much good.
Hartman Rector, Jr., CR 10/72:171

It is not half so important for our neighbors to know that we are honest as it is for ourselves to know it.
Franklin D. Richards (1821, 1849-1899), CR 4/98:18

It is just as easy for an honest man to be honest as it is for a dishonest man to be dishonest. It is just as easy for a faithful man to be faithful as it is for an unfaithful man to be unfaithful.
Sterling W. Sill, CR 10/62:38

Honesty is not subject to law.
Joseph Smith, HC 6:206

The Savior must have been an honorable and honest

carpenter, or he never could have merited the position he afterwards occupied.
Lorenzo Snow, JD 18:301

Honesty cannot become a national, a world-wide virtue, unless it becomes a primal part of the thinking, the actions, and the character of the individual.
Joseph L. Wirthlin, CR 10/49:99

HOPE

No matter what your past has been, you have a spotless future.
Hugh B. Brown, CR 10/69:103

> *See also:* Faith

HUMILITY

There is no position in this Church that is not bigger than the man that holds it.
Hugh B. Brown, CR 10/61:86

Humility is a state of mind, and not a condition, necessarily, of finances.
Sylvester Q. Cannon, CR 4/31:16

Humility is inward strength outwardly expressed in good works.
Charles A. Callis, CR 4/42:42

Meekness is a condition of voluntary humility.
Alvin R. Dyer, CR 10/70:151

No man is so wise that he cannot benefit by talking things out with others.
Richard L. Evans, CR 4/70:16

I can do anything I am set apart to do, if I have the spirit of my appointment and am humble and prayerful.
J. Golden Kimball, CR 4/18:133

I do not want a rosewood casket. I am willing to be buried among the people in a plain casket, and all I want inscribed on the headboard of my grave is that I have been true to this Church and to the priesthood of God, and have walked in the footsteps of my father.
  J. Golden Kimball, CR 4/05:53

I have discovered in my short career that I don't amount to very much; that all that I have tried to do within myself I have failed in.
  J. Golden Kimball, CR 10/97:50

No man ever became great who was not humble.
  Anthon H. Lund, CR 4/01:22

If you were to take away from me that which properly belonged to somebody else, there wouldn't be very much of me left.
  Sterling W. Sill, CR 10/74:85

The path of humility is always the path of safety.
  George Albert Smith, CR 4/23:78

I do not believe that any man has discovered any principle in science, or art; in mechanism, or mathematics, or anything else, that God did not know before he did.
  Joseph F. Smith, CR 4/02:85

Any man who has not enough of the spirit of humility to be governed is not fit to govern. A man who cannot be led is not fit to lead.
  Abraham O. Woodruff, CR 4/01:12

All the learning and knowledge upon the face of the earth cannot, of themselves, make or produce a spear of grass, or the smallest leaf upon a tree.
  Brigham Young, JD 3:276

HUMOR

A wholesome sense of humor will be a safety valve that will enable you to apply the lighter touch to

heavy problems and to learn some lessons in problem solving that "sweat and tears" often fail to dissolve.
Hugh B. Brown, CR 4/68:100

HUSBANDS

A woman happy with her husband is better for her children than a hundred books on child welfare.
Anon. Harold B. Lee, ACR 8/72:91

No sane woman would hesitate to give submission to her own really righteous husband in everything.
Spencer W. Kimball, CR 4/65:63

Polish your husband as best you can while you have him with you here and then hope that the Lord will continue the process to aid you even beyond the veil.
Harold B. Lee, ACR 8/73:55

"Nagging wives" cannot nag their husbands into doing anything that is worthwhile.
Stephen L Richards, CR 4/58:96

If any man ought to be damned in this world, it is the man that will abandon the mother of his children.
Joseph F. Smith, CR 4/17:7

See also: Family, Fatherhood, Man

HYPOCRISY

No man can stand in this Church, or retain the Spirit of God and continue in a course of hypocrisy for any length of time.
George Q. Cannon, JD 18:84

Men and women think evil thoughts, they give place to angry feelings; and they think it a meritorious act, and pride themselves upon their conduct because they give them utterance instead of quenching them! . . . It is not hypocrisy to quench the evil thoughts that arise in our minds.
George Q. Cannon, JD 21:78

I love that man better who swears a stream as long as
my arm yet deals justice to his neighbors and
mercifully deals his substance to the poor, than the
long, smooth-faced hypocrite.
  Joseph Smith, HC 5:401

None of us need think that we shall be benefitted by
covering up our uncleanness and expect that we shall
be sanctified by the outer ordinances of the temple of
our God, when the inner man is corrupt.
  Erastus Snow, CR 4/80:90

Don't despise the pure gold of religion simply because
the devil has made a counterfeit of it in hypocrisy.
  Rulon S. Wells, CR 10/22:122

IDEAS

The kind of emphasis that is given to an idea is
sometimes about as important as the idea itself.
  Sterling W. Sill, CR 10/71:98

If I were asked to give the best idea of which I am
capable, it would be that we should get out of the junk
business and then start laying up treasures in heaven.
  Sterling W. Sill, CR 10/73:78

In the greatest sermon that was ever preached, the
greatest man who ever lived gave what was probably
the wisest counsel that has ever been given when he
said that we should lay up for ourselves treasures in
heaven. And that is probably our most profitable idea.
  Sterling W. Sill, CR 10/73:77

  See also: Thoughts

IDLENESS

Why delude ourselves into thinking that a third of us
may live in idleness and all of us be better off? If a
third may be idle, and all be better off than now, then
why not a half idle and increase the prosperity; and if

half, why not two-thirds, and if two-thirds, then all of us idle and have every man a millionaire, and nobody working.
J. Reuben Clark, Jr., CR 4/37:26

During the whole range of man's existence there has never yet been any plan by which men may live righteously in idleness.
J. Reuben Clark, Jr., CR 10/36:112

I know of nothing that is so degenerating and so dangerous as idleness, for the brain will seek out mischief.
Francis M. Lyman, CR 10/09:19

There is nothing more dangerous than idleness. . . . In labor there is salvation; in labor there is safety.
Francis M. Lyman, CR 10/07:15

No man that is idle can be honest and virtuous and of use in the community. No woman that is an idler can be clean and sweet.
John Henry Smith, CR 10/09:23

I think about the meanest being on this earth is a lazy man.
Reed Smoot, CR 10/09:70

If there is any one thing that will bring trouble to the children of the Latter-day Saints more than another it is . . . to . . . raise them up in idleness.
Reed Smoot, CR 10/04:48

Inactivity is death. Wherever there is a body of people upon the face of the earth that has nothing to do, that quorum or body will die spiritually. The spirit of God will not be with men who are inactive. The spirit of God is a spirit of progression.
Abraham O. Woodruff, CR 4/98:21

Perhaps the faith of some people is such that they think the Lord will send down an angel with a loaf of bread under one arm and a leg of bacon under the

other—that an angel will be sent from some other world with bread ready buttered for them to eat.
Brigham Young, JD 11:105

IGNORANCE

Ignorance is expensive.
Hartman Rector, Jr., CR 4/71:102

There are a great many wise men and women too in our midst who are too wise to be taught; therefore they must die in their ignorance, and in the resurrection they will find their mistake.
Joseph Smith, HC 5:424

Ignorance is the mother of crime.
Abraham O. Woodruff, CR 4/02:79

IMMORALITY

The easiest way to destroy a man's faith is to destroy his morality.
Melvin J. Ballard, CR 4/29:65

You cannot build a happy home; you cannot build a happy married life on the foundation of immorality.
Ezra Taft Benson, ACR 8/74:68

The warm sunlight of love will not rise out of a swamp of immorality.
Gordon B. Hinckley, CR 10/70:66

The greatest menace or enemy which the Church of Christ has to combat is intemperance and sexual sin.
Anthony W. Ivins, CR 4/10:113

The trends of permissiveness toward immorality are destroying the moral fabric of our generation.
Spencer W. Kimball, CR 10/74:7

Immorality is totally selfish.
Spencer W. Kimball, CR 4/74:8

The so-called "new morality" is but the old immorality in a new setting.
Spencer W. Kimball, CR 4/67:64

When a Latter-day Saint becomes immoral, he ceases to be a Latter-day Saint.
Francis M. Lyman, CR 10/15:74

One of the evidences that there is a God is the great scourge and curse that he places upon men and women who are immoral.
LeGrand Richards, CR 4/40:134

You can't cancel off a little immorality with a little industry, or a little dishonesty with a little ability, or a little atheism with a few good intentions.
Sterling W. Sill, CR 10/71:99

An unvirtuous youth or maiden is like fruit without flavor, or the flower that hath no fragrance, or the salt that hath lost its savor.
Rulon S. Wells, CR 4/22:143

The devil is not opposed to immorality.
Abraham O. Woodruff, CR 10/00:55

See also: Adultery, Chastity, Sex

IMPROVEMENT

All improvement comes as a result of repentance.
Eldred G. Smith, CR 4/54:87

Who is there who has reached that point in life where he can afford to allow himself to stop growing or to stop improving?
John H. Vandenberg, CR 10/72:23

See also: Progress, Success

INDIAN (See Lamanite)

INDIFFERENCE

There is one thing more serious than merely to "not believe," and that is to "not care."
Sterling W. Sill, CR 10/55:46

The sin of indifference is one of the worst things we have to contend with today.
Reed Smoot, CR 10/07:57

The great enemy of the kingdom of God is indifference.
Rulon S. Wells, CR 4/08:113

INDIVIDUALITY

An appreciation of diversification is the basis of unity.
Theodore M. Burton, CR 10/69:34

There is a class of men who consider everybody disloyal who does not dance to their tunes, and who does not re-echo the sentiments which they express and seem to entertain.
George Q. Cannon, JD 18:6

I am a thorough convert myself to the idea that it is not possible for all men to see alike.
Heber J. Grant, CR 10/19:19

I am very doubtful if a man can be saved in the kingdom of God who has no individuality, and does not assert his agency, because salvation is an individual work.
J. Golden Kimball, CR 4/07:78

The collapse of systems is always preceded by the collapse of individuals.
Neal A. Maxwell, CR 4/75:150

There are some who have never reasoned carefully along the line of the possibility of two men, for example, looking at things from different points of view, and seeing different images, and yet both seeing

the truth.
James E. Talmage, CR 10/20:65

See also: Agency, Freedom

INSPIRATION

The Latter-day Saints are safe as long as they listen to the voice of inspiration.
Matthias F. Cowley, CR 4/99:10

One of the most fruitful sources of spiritual education lies in the thoughts which arise in our own hearts.
George F. Richards, CR 10/06:66

It matters very little what we are engaged in, it is impossible for us to do right without the guidance of the Almighty.
John Taylor, JD 13:221

When the Lord speaks to me or to you, it will be in a method and manner justified by our preparation, our gifts, our powers.
Orson F. Whitney, CR 4/10:60

See also: Holy Ghost, Revelation

INSTINCT

There is in man not only an instinct, but also a divinity that strives to push him onward and upward. The sense is universal, and at some time in his life every man is conscious of possessing it.
David O. McKay, CR 4/68:91

Every instinct in us is for a wise purpose in God when properly regulated and restrained and guided by the Holy Spirit and kept within its proper legitimate bounds.
Erastus Snow, JD 26:217

See also: Nature

INTEGRITY

A true measure of one's devotion to a principle is measured not by what he professes, but by what he manifests—day by day.
    ElRay L. Christiansen, CR 10/52:55

The key to a unified Church is a unified soul.
    Howard W. Hunter, CR 4/76:157

If a man profess faith in God and has integrity, he will adhere to God's commandments.
    Anthony W. Ivins, CR 4/16:58

We do not believe in situation-itis.
    Spencer W. Kimball, CR 4/75:162

The foundation of a noble character is integrity.
    David O. McKay, CR 4/64:6

If I had to make a choice, which I ought not to have to make, between talent and integrity, I would choose integrity and virtue, for without them we are lost.
    Stephen L Richards, CR 10/53:101

INTELLIGENCE

Intelligence is that which enables one to wisely meet the situations of life without education; whereas, education is that which helps one to meet the situations of life without intelligence.
    Anon. Stephen L Richards, CR 4/38:23

Intelligence and knowledge, of the right kind, walks ever close to religion.
    J. Golden Kimball, CR 10/26:131

Real intelligence is the creative use of knowledge, not merely an accumulation of facts.
    Spencer W. Kimball, CR 10/68:130

It takes just as high an order of intelligence to comprehend and assimilate spiritual truth and divine

law as it does to master the equations and formulas in the field of secular education.
Stephen L Richards, CR 4/49:139

Intelligence is the power to grasp and assimilate the fundamental, essential truths of God and the universe.
Stephen L Richards, CR 4/25:33

The mind or the intelligence which man possesses is co-equal with God himself.
Joseph Smith, HC 6:310

> *See also:* Knowledge

INTELLIGENCES

Intelligences are begotten spirits, and they partake of the nature of him who begets them. . . . A created thing may not partake of the nature of him who creates it.
B. H. Roberts, CR 4/04:18

> *See also:* Premortal Existence

INTENTIONS

Anyone with good intentions will never be found doing anything very wrong.
Rulon S. Wells, CR 4/10:22

Hell is not paved with good intentions; it would be more appropriate to say it is paved with evil intentions.
Rulon S. Wells, CR 4/10:22

> *See also:* Desires, Motives

INTROSPECTION

I believe that each of us needs a spiritual checkup just about as often as we need a physical checkup.
ElRay L. Christiansen, CR 10/59:68

The only measure of true greatness is how close a man can become like Jesus.
Ezra Taft Benson, CR 10/72:53

Though Rome had her Caesars, her master artists, and her geniuses; though Athens had her conquerors, her statesmen, and her philosophers; though Egypt had her pompous dictators and her unrelenting Pharaohs, it remained for little Bethlehem and later for Nazareth and Galilee to give to this world its most transcendent personage.
Hugh B. Brown, CR 10/60:92

The greatest hero, if you will, who has ever lived is the Savior of mankind, Jesus Christ.
Victor L. Brown, CR 10/70:124

People need recreation, need to be achieving, need to contribute; but if these come at the cost of friendship with Christ, the price is much too high.
Marion D. Hanks, CR 4/72:127

On Calvary he was the dying Jesus. From the tomb he emerged the living Christ. The cross had been the bitter fruit of Judas' betrayal, the summary of Peter's denial. The empty tomb now became the testimony of his divinity, the assurance of eternal life, the answer to Job's unanswered question: "If a man die, shall he live again?" (Job 14:14.)
Gordon B. Hinckley, CR 4/75:138

Christ could not have been humanity's greatest moral teacher unless he was in very deed the Son of God.
Heber J. Grant, CR 4/27:9

The name Jesus Christ and what it represents have been plowed deep into the history of the world, never to be uprooted.
Spencer W. Kimball, CR 4/75:3

Jesus' grip on himself was also mankind's hold on the

future.
Neal A. Maxwell, CR 4/76:40

No son ever complemented his father so gracefully, honored his father so constantly, or trusted his father so completely as did Jesus.
Neal A. Maxwell, CR 4/76:41

I accept Jesus Christ as the personification of human perfection.
David O. McKay, CR 10/65:144

There is no Savior but Jesus, and he saves only in his own strait and narrow way and not according to manmade creeds and rituals.
Mark E. Petersen, CR 4/73:159

Who in the heavens above and on the earth beneath had a better right to pronounce judgment upon the churches of the world than the Savior of the world?
LeGrand Richards, CR 4/74:170

No wholesome reverence for the Lord will ever come except there be an understanding and comprehension of him.
Stephen L Richards, CR 10/24:65

The most inspiring thing about the life of Jesus was not his ability to quiet the storm or control the tempest, but absolute control of himself.
Sterling W. Sill, CR 10/63:78

The Redeemer of mankind was more than a good man who came into the world to teach us ethics.
George Albert Smith, CR 10/21:39

The Lord cannot always be known by the thunder of His voice, by the display of His glory or by the manifestation of His power.
Joseph Smith, HC 5:31

Christ is the great prototype.
Joseph Fielding Smith, CR 10/70:92

The most important and most significant of all events
that have happened in the history and life of mankind
are the birth, life, death, and resurrection of our Lord
and Savior, Jesus Christ, the Only Begotten of God
the Eternal Father.
  N. Eldon Tanner, CR 4/66:134

The life of a God was the price of the world's freedom,
and that price was paid by him who is called Jesus the
Nazarene.
  Orson F. Whitney, CR 10/13:98

The death on Calvary was no more the ending of that
divine career, than the birth at Bethlehem was its
beginning.
  Orson F. Whitney, CR 4/27:101

  See also: Atonement, Easter, God, Sacrament

JOSEPH SMITH

The scriptures did not come so much from Joseph
Smith as they did through him.
  Boyd K. Packer, CR 4/74:137

The whole world is fermenting with the leaven that
God planted when he brought this work into the earth
through the Prophet Joseph Smith.
  B. H. Roberts, CR 4/03:13

No man had so much as heard of the prophet Joseph
Smith but what the "still small voice" whispered to
him that he was a true prophet.
  B. H. Roberts, CR 4/05:44

I will become a smooth and polished shaft in the
quiver of the Almighty.
  Joseph Smith, HC 5:401

I am going like a lamb to the slaughter, but I am calm
as a summer's morning. I have a conscience void of
offense toward God and toward all men. If they take

my life I shall die an innocent man, and my blood shall cry from the ground for vengeance, and it shall be said of me "He was murdered in cold blood."
Joseph Smith, HC 6:555

JOY

Pleasure, in my mind, is essentially a gratification of one of the senses. Happiness seems to center in a kind of contentment born of good fortune or of some fortuitous circumstance. But joy reveals a certain spiritual exaltation.
Adam S. Bennion, CR 4/55:110

The man who expects to find a fulness of joy in the light and frivolous pleasures of the world or in matters pertaining strictly to the world will be sadly disappointed.
Rudger Clawson, CR 10/32:10

No man could have permanent joy without salvation.
Rudger Clawson, CR 4/31:19

When joy is produced in the soul of man by the doing of things claimed to be revealed from the Lord, it is an evidence that the thing is right.
Joseph W. McMurrin, CR 4/09:96

There is no joy that can compare with that of a missionary who has been made the instrument for the salvation of a soul.
Orson F. Whitney, CR 4/18:73

See also: Happiness, Pleasure

JUDGMENT

If there are to be distinctions among us, they must not be based upon our financial condition, but rather upon the principle of righteousness.
Rudger Clawson, CR 4/99:4

Thank God we are not to be judged by the opinions of
our fellows, but by the work that we do.
  Heber J. Grant, CR 10/07:26

We will not be judged by the sermons we preach or
the sermons we hear. We will not be judged by the
number of meetings we attend. Nor will we be judged
by the prayers we utter or those we hear. If we are
satisfied with these things only, we are like the tree
that is satisfied with being cultivated and irrigated
and with putting forth leaves but bearing no fruit.
  Richard R. Lyman, CR 4/21:145

The mere fact that we receive the ordinances in no
sense guarantees that we will receive these rewards.
  Bruce R. McConkie, CR 10/55:13

No man will rise high who jeers at sacred things.
  David O. McKay, CR 10/55:91

The measuring stick is not someone else's
accomplishment, but your own capabilities.
  Franklin D. Richards (1900, 1960-   ), ACR 8/72:25

Someone once painted a famous picture entitled
"Christ before Pilate." It represents Jesus being
judged and condemned by the people of the world he
came to save. But someday another picture may be
painted entitled "Pilate before Christ."
  Sterling W. Sill, CR 10/68:137

The ultimate judgment for every man will be on the
simplest terms, and most certainly on what each has
done to bless other people in a quiet, unassuming way.
  Robert L. Simpson, CR 4/73:19

A man is his own tormentor and his own condemner.
  Joseph Smith, HC 6:314

The disappointment of hopes and expectations at the
resurrection would be indescribably dreadful.
  Joseph Smith, HC 6:51

No man is capable of judging a matter, in council, unless his own heart is pure.
Joseph Smith, HC 2:25

When we come to stand before the bar of God, to be judged out of the things which are written in the books, we may find a difference between those things which are written in the books here and the things which are written in the books there.
Joseph F. Smith, CR 4/99:68

The further out of line or out of tune we ourselves are, the more we are inclined to look for error or weaknesses in others.
N. Eldon Tanner, CR 4/72:56

When you judge a man or woman, judge the intentions of the heart. It is not by words, particularly, nor by actions, that men will be judged in the great day of the Lord; but, in connection with words and actions, the sentiments and intentions of the heart will be taken, and by these will men be judged.
Brigham Young, JD 8:10

When you know the intention of the act performed, you will then know how to judge the act.
Brigham Young, JD 8:37

We should judge all people not by their mistakes but by the abundance of their powers.
Levi Edgar Young, CR 10/53:66

See also: Justice, Plan of Salvation, Punishment, Rewards

JUSTICE

A basic cornerstone of true justice is compassion.
Robert L. Simpson, CR 4/72:32-33

In my feelings I am always ready to die for the protection of the weak and oppressed in their just rights.
Joseph Smith, HC 6:57

See also: Judgment

117

KEYS

Where the oracles of God are not, there the kingdom
of God is not.
Joseph Smith, HC 5:257

I will inform you that it is contrary to the economy of
God for any member of the Church, or any one, to
receive instruction for those in authority, higher than
themselves.
Joseph Smith, HC 1:338

Any man who says he is a teacher or preacher of
righteousness, and denies the spirit of prophecy, is a
liar, and the truth is not in him; and by this key false
teachers and impostors may be detected.
Joseph Smith, HC 5:215-16

I make this broad declaration, that whenever God
gives a vision of an image, or beast, or figure of any
kind, he always holds himself responsible to give a
revelation or interpretation of the meaning thereof,
otherwise we are not responsible or accountable for
our belief in it.
Joseph Smith, HC 5:343

I have a key by which I understand the scriptures. I
enquire, what was the question which drew out the
answer, or caused Jesus to utter the parable?
Joseph Smith, HC 5:261

As a rule, the man that does not pay his tithing and
that does not keep the word of wisdom is the man that
is everlastingly quizzing and asking questions about
things he does not understand.
Joseph F. Smith, CR 10/16:7

KINDNESS

Every kind act that we perform for one of our Father's
children is but a permanent investment made by us
that will bear eternal dividends.
George Albert Smith, CR 4/14:13

Our lives are ruled by a schedule and appointments while the Christian acts of kindness wait—ofttimes in vain.

A. Theodore Tuttle, CR 10/71:95

KINGDOM OF GOD

Whenever there has been a righteous man on earth unto whom God revealed His word and gave power and authority to administer in his name, and where there is a priest of God— a minister who has power and authority from God to administer in the ordinances of the gospel and officate in the priesthood of God, there is the kingdom of God.

Joseph Smith, HC 5:256

It will not be by sword or gun that this kingdom will roll on.

Joseph Smith, HC 6:365

Where there is no kingdom of God there is no salvation.

Joseph Smith, HC 5:257

No man is king of the kingdom of God.

Joseph F. Smith, CR 4/16:6

See also: Church, Mormonism

KNOWLEDGE

Every time I have to do anything, I know that I could do it better if I only knew more. The limit of my power is the limit of my knowledge and understanding; if I can extend the scope of these, I can grow in power, because truly, knowledge is power.

Albert E. Bowen, CR 10/43:81-82

Man's flight through life is sustained by the power of his knowledge.

Hugh B. Brown, CR 4/68:100

Spiritual insight is as real as scientific insight. Indeed, it is but a higher manifestation of the same thing.
  Hugh B. Brown, CR 4/67:49

A good brain and the skill of man's right hand can produce wonders.
  George Q. Cannon, JD 22:275

Obedience must often precede knowledge.
  J. Reuben Clark, Jr., CR 4/50:181

There is spiritual learning just as there is material learning, and the one without the other is not complete; yet, speaking for myself, if I could have only one sort of learning, that which I would take would be the learning of the spirit, because in the hereafter I shall have opportunity in the eternities which are to come to get the other, and without spiritual learning here my handicaps in the hereafter would be all but overwhelming.
  J. Reuben Clark, Jr., CR 4/34:94

Knowledge is the handmaid of intelligence and priceless beyond all words, and knowledge implies within it not alone learning but experience.
  J. Reuben Clark, Jr., CR 4/34:94

We need to know more, but also we need more to use more of what we do know.
  Richard L. Evans, CR 4/57:12

If we shall miss realizing our highest happiness and possibilities and opportunities and progress and peace and development, it will not be because of what we do not know, it will be because of what we ignore.
  Richard L. Evans, CR 10/52:126

Knowledge is absolutely of no value, except to condemn us before God, unless we live up to that knowledge.
  Heber J. Grant, CR 10/14:78

The man who neglects to discipline and train his mind in the science of religion knows but little about God or angels, or the glory of the sanctified. What little he does understand, he has borrowed from the labours and toils of others.

Orson Hyde, JD 6:374

I have learned that appointment does not give a man knowledge.

J. Golden Kimball, CR 4/10:58

The knowledge of the spiritual will not come to an individual without effort any more than will the secular knowledge or college degrees.

Spencer W. Kimball, CR 10/68:129

Testimony and knowledge of God cannot be lost except through transgression.

Henry D. Moyle, CR 4/63:46

We believe the greater, the more general our knowledge is, the freer we become and the more intelligent the use we make of our free agency.

Henry D. Moyle, CR 4/58:64

We live in a world where almost no one knows anything for sure.

Hartman Rector, Jr., CR 4/75:81

People do not really care how much you know until they know how much you care.

Hartman Rector, Jr., CR 10/73:136

If we were to do as well as we know, our salvation would be secure.

George F. Richards, CR 4/36:77

Perfect wisdom can come only from perfect knowledge.

B. H. Roberts, CR 10/25:147

There is no knowledge other than knowledge of the things of God that will save us.

Marion G. Romney, CR 4/62:18

Fortunately for us there is no flaming sword guarding

the tree of knowledge, and each one of us may eat to
his heart's content.
  Sterling W. Sill, CR 4/73:144

The opinions of men, so far as I am concerned, are to ·
me as the crackling of thorns under the pot, or the
whistling of the wind.
  Joseph Smith, HC 5:402

When we have power to put all enemies under our feet
in this world, and a knowledge to triumph over all evil
spirits in the world to come, then we are saved.
  Joseph Smith, HC 5:387

✳A man is saved no faster than he gets knowledge.
  Joseph Smith, HC 4:588

Knowledge through our Lord and Savior Jesus Christ
is the grand key that unlocks the glories and mysteries
of the kingdom of heaven.
  Joseph Smith, HC 5:389

In knowledge there is power. God has more power
than all other beings, because he has greater
knowledge; and hence he knows how to subject all
other beings to him. He has power over all.
  Joseph Smith, HC 5:340

If a man has knowledge, he can be saved; although, if
he has been guilty of great sins, he will be punished for
them.
  Joseph Smith, HC 6:314

The things of God are of deep import; and time, and
experience, and careful and ponderous and solemn
thoughts can only find them out.
  Joseph Smith, HC 3:295

We cannot keep all the commandments without first
knowing them, and we cannot expect to know all, or
more than we now know unless we comply with or
keep those we have already received.
  Joseph Smith, HC 5:135

✳ The principle of knowledge is the principle of
salvation.
Joseph Smith, HC 5:387

I believe that it is the destiny of this people to become
the leaders in education, in knowledge, in
understanding and in all those accomplishments
which go to make the perfect man and the perfect
woman.
Rulon S. Wells, CR 4/10:21

Curiously enough, our wealth of modern, man-made
knowledge sheds little light upon the meaning of life,
unless interpreted in the light of revealed religion.
John A. Widtsoe, CR 4/25:27

Knowledge unused is scarcely worth the having; but
knowledge once used leaps into light and life and
becomes a bright flame to guide and to help man.
John A. Widtsoe, CR 10/21:46

Every once in a while, as we journey through life, we
meet some man who is rich in knowledge, but uses his
knowledge only as an ornament on his intellectual
mantel-shelf simply to be looked at.
John A. Widtsoe, CR 10/21:46

> *See also:* Belief, Education, Faith, Mind, Testimony,
> Wisdom

LAMANITE

The day of the Lamanite is come, and tomorrow will
be even better.
Spencer W. Kimball, CR 10/65:71

LANGUAGE

Oh, Lord, deliver us in due time from the little,
narrow prison, almost as it were, total darkness of
paper, pen and ink;—and a crooked, broken, scattered
and imperfect language.
Joseph Smith, HC 1:299

There are so many tongues spoken among men; the
world is a Babel; but of the tongues used by the Lord
in his communication with men he selects for each
occasion the language that they ought to understand.
  James E. Talmage, CR 10/32:77

Our language is meagre when we speak of heavenly
things, because it is made for earthly beings.
  John Taylor, JD 11:75

LATTER DAYS

We live in an age of deceit.
  Ezra Taft Benson, CR 4/72:52

To the Church has been assigned the honor of the title
role in God's great drama of the last days.
  B. H. Roberts, CR 4/03:13

It is a day of warning and not of many words.
  Joseph Smith, HC 3:384

The servants of God will not have gone over the
nations of the Gentiles, with a warning voice, until the
destroying angel will commence to waste the
inhabitants of the earth.
  Joseph Smith, HC 2:263

The saints have not too much time to save and redeem
their dead, and gather together their living relatives,
that they may be saved also, before the earth will be
smitten, and the consumption decreed falls upon the
world.
  Joseph Smith, HC 6:184

This generation is as corrupt as the generation of the
Jews that crucified Christ; and if he were here today,
and should preach the same doctrine he did then, they
would put him to death.
  Joseph Smith, HC 6:58

The last days are here and now.
  N. Eldon Tanner, CR 10/68:46

We are now enjoying the very things that Prophets prophesied of as they looked through the dark vista of ages unborn and contemplated these blessings that we enjoy.
John Taylor, JD 5:264

See also: Dispensation, Millennium

LATTER-DAY SAINTS

A real Latter-day Saint, is a good husband, he is a good father, he is a good neighbor, he is a good citizen, and a good man all round; and it takes a good Latter-day Saint to be a first class everything else.
Joseph F. Smith, CR 4/10:8

I hope you will draw the distinction between Latter-day Saints and latter-day devils.
Joseph F. Smith, CR 4/03:74

See also: Church, Mormons, Saint

LAW

There have to be standards and they must be enforced, but our love must be unconditional.
Marion D. Hanks, CR 10/71:119

Without just laws by which society may be controlled and the rights of the people protected, and honest, conscientious men to administer them, the Church cannot exist.
Anthony W. Ivins, CR 4/19:81

Has puny, irresponsible, presumptuous man dared to change the laws of God?
Spencer W. Kimball, CR 4/75:161

Every Latter-day Saint should sustain, honor and obey the constitutional law of the land in which he lives.
Spencer W. Kimball, CR 4/74:5

When one sets himself up to make his own rules and presumes to know no law but his own, he is but echoing the plan of Satan.
Harold B. Lee, CR 4/72:121

To be honest means that we are in harmony with divine law.
David O. McKay, CR 10/08:108

There is no order without law.
Stephen L Richards, CR 10/54:82

Law and order is the basis of the priesthood.
Robert L. Simpson, CR 10/70:101

Wicked spirits have their bounds, limits, and law by which they are governed or controlled, and know their future destiny.
Joseph Smith, HC 4:576

It will hurt no good man to have good and wholesome laws.
Rulon S. Wells, CR 10/09:113

Law is made for the lawless. Let the Saints live their religion, and there is not a law that can justly infringe upon them. They are subject to the powers that be, by living so pure that no law can touch them.
Brigham Young, JD 8:140

LEADERSHIP

The hand that holds the reins is not the power that pulls the load.
Anon. A. Theodore Tuttle, CR 4/72:150

The first element of true leadership is faith in God and obedience to his principles.
Samuel O. Bennion, CR 4/39:28

There are too many favor-currying little men sloshing around in positions requiring big men of unwavering

integrity to fill them.
Albert E. Bowen, CR 10/46:50

An office or title will not erase a fault nor guarantee a virtue.
Hugh B. Brown, CR 4/62:88

The best evidence that a man is unfit for Church office is the fact that he wants it.
J. Reuben Clark, Jr., CR 4/40:72

There is no appointment in this Church, that I know of, that is absolutely permanent, excepting the Holy Priesthood, which we are called to hold.
Rudger Clawson, CR 10/01:65

No man, no matter what may be his natural attainments, if he does not enjoy the Spirit of the living God, if his life is not circumspect, squared by the principles and doctrines of the Son of God, is a well educated Latter-day Saint, he does not enjoy the true light, he is not a safe man to follow.
Matthias F. Cowley, CR 10/97:55

The kingdom is no stronger nor better than its officers.
William J. Critchlow, Jr., CR 10/63:28

The price of leadership is loneliness.
Gordon B. Hinckley, ACR 8/73:88

It is impossible to honor the priesthood and not honor the vessel that holds it.
Heber C. Kimball, JD 11:80

Buckskin men are not developed indoors.
J. Golden Kimball, CR 10/12:28

We need revelation for the calling of officers in the Church. Men should not be called merely through impression.
J. Golden Kimball, CR 4/10:55

It matters not what position a man holds in the Church, if he uses any unrighteous dominion it is

amen to the priesthood that he holds.
J. Golden Kimball, CR 4/07:81

Even if the priesthood holders of our Heavenly Father
are headed in the right direction, if they are men
without momentum they will have too little influence.
Spencer W. Kimball, CR 4/76:69

It would be a poor lighthouse that gave off a different
signal to guide every ship entering a harbor.
Spencer W. Kimball, CR 4/76:7

The absolute test of the divinity of the calling of any
officer in the Church is this: Is he in harmony with the
brethren of that body to which he belongs?
Harold B. Lee, CR 4/66:66

You cannot lift another soul until you are standing on
higher ground than he is. . . . You cannot light a fire in
another soul unless it is burning in your own soul.
Harold B. Lee, CR 4/73:178

The only true record that will ever be made of my
service in my new calling will be the record that I may
have written in the hearts and lives of those with
whom I have served and labored, within and without
the Church.
Harold B. Lee, CR 10/72:19

Every man who will be called to a high place in this
Church will have to pass tests not devised by human
hands, by which our Father numbers them as a united
group of leaders willing to follow the prophets of the
living God and be loyal and true as witnesses and
exemplars of the truths they teach.
Harold B. Lee, CR 4/50:101

It is not position in the Church that confers spiritual
gifts.
Bruce R. McConkie, CR 10/69:82

In leadership cleverness is not as important as content.
. . . Charisma and dash are not as vital as character

and doctrine.
Neal A. Maxwell, CR 4/75:150-51

The most worthy calling in life is that in which man
can serve best his fellow man.
David O. McKay, CR 4/61:131

It is to the leaders of the Church that members turn
when they have not yet learned to discern inspiration.
Boyd K. Packer, ACR 8/74:21

The man who is not willing to labor as a deacon is not
fit to be a President.
Charles W. Penrose, CR 4/04:73

Holding a particular office in the Church will never
save a person.
Marion G. Romney, CR 4/73:116-17

The power to lead, possessed by every parent, is also
the power to mislead. The power to mislead is the
power to destroy; it is the power to cause eternal
suffering.
Sterling W. Sill, CR 4/60:67

Our great leadership is of small consequence if we
stumble in our followship.
Sterling W. Sill, CR 4/62:14

It is not necessary that a man should be a member of
the Quorum of the Twelve, or the Presidency of the
Church, in order to obtain the greatest blessings in the
kingdom of our Heavenly Father. These are but offices
required in the Church.
George Albert Smith, CR 4/19:42-43

Handsome men are not apt to be wise and
strong-minded men.
Joseph Smith, HC 5:389

There is not a man holding any position of authority
in the Church who can perform his duty as he should
in any other spirit than in the spirit of fatherhood and

brotherhood toward those over whom he presides.
Joseph F. Smith, CR 4/15:5

It does not matter what office we hold as long as we
are true and faithful to our obligations.
Joseph Fielding Smith, CR 10/70:91

It requires more energy and more strength of purpose
in a man to follow out the counsel of one who is just
above him than it is to follow a man that is a long way
ahead of him.
Lorenzo Snow, JD 5:315

God tries people according to the position they
occupy.
John Taylor, JD 24:197-98

We need strong leaders of good character in all
places—leaders who are examples of integrity,
dependability, and righteousness.
N. Eldon Tanner, CR 10/74:122

Every position in the Church is greater than the
person who holds it.
Henry D. Taylor, ACR 8/71:148

The teacher, or deacon that fulfills his duties is a great
deal more honorable than a president or any of the
twelve that does not.
John Taylor, JD 21:209

There never was a man in the Church of God that
received the spirit of any calling whereunto he was
called until he started to administer in that calling.
John W. Taylor, CR 10/00:31

When the servants of God, filled with the Holy Ghost
nominate a man, and the Holy Ghost in the hearts of
the people testifies that that is the choice of God, it is
His choice. It is impossible for a mistake to be made.
Orson F. Whitney, CR 10/05:92

No man can be a safe leader who does not love truth

above all else.
John A. Widtsoe, CR 10/42:74

He that most desires an office is the least fit for it.
Perhaps I made a mistake in that declaration, for
though on general principles it is true, it may not be
true in every case.
Brigham Young, JD 15:17

When the Lord God has wanted to train great leaders
for his eternal purposes, he has not hesitated to choose
boys, call them, anoint them, prepare them, and then
when grown send them forth to their allotted destiny.
S. Dilworth Young, CR 10/74:130

See also: Church, Priesthood, Prophets, Responsibility

LIBERTY

Human liberty is the mainspring of human progress.
Ezra Taft Benson, CR 10/62:14

Liberty is a thing of the spirit. A man must nourish it
and cherish it in his heart as he does love for his wife
and children. Except for its manifestations as a quality
in human life it has no existence. Governments cannot
confer it; they can only protect the individual in the
enjoyment of it.
Albert E. Bowen, CR 10/40:125

There can be no progress without liberty.
Henry D. Moyle, CR 4/59:97

All the systems that may be devised, all of the
governments that can be constructed, will not bring
liberty to mankind if the true principles of liberty are
not in the hearts of the people.
Stephen L Richards, CR 10/19:105

Dear as peace is to me, it is not so dear that I would
purchase it at the sacrifice of human rights and
human liberty.
B. H. Roberts, CR 10/12:34

The same principle which would trample upon the rights of the Latter-day Saints would trample upon the rights of the Roman Catholics, or of any other denomination who may be unpopular and too weak to defend themselves.

Joseph Smith, HC 5:498

It is a love of liberty which inspires my soul—and religious liberty to the whole of the human race.

Joseph Smith, HC 5:498

Sacred is the memory of that blood which bought for us our liberty.

Joseph Smith, HC 3:9

Man is an independent being in his agency, to do right or wrong, and has the liberty of doing as he pleases; but I qualify this by saying that he has not the right to do wrong or to infringe upon the rights of another individual. This is the law of society, and it is also the law of heaven.

Daniel H. Wells, JD 9:100

See also: Freedom

LIFE

The whole purpose and object of life is to achieve individual perfection through the unfolding of individual potentialities and the ripening of all the virtues.

Albert E. Bowen, CR 4/38:9

Don't gamble with life. It is all we have.

Richard L. Evans, CR 10/71:34

This life is a school, and commencement day to us will be when the battle of this life is o'er and we commence anew to travel on forever. Then if we can pass an examination, we are welcomed back into the presence of our Heavenly Father, because we have been true and faithful.

Heber J. Grant, CR 10/14:77-78

This life is but an interlude between two eternities.
   Thorpe B. Isaacson, CR 4/61:62

Life is made up not of great sacrifices or duties, but of little things in which smiles and kindness and small obligations given habitually are what win and preserve the heart and secure comfort.
   David O. McKay, CR 10/56:6

The whole purpose and end of existence is *life,* and to obtain in that life, *peace.*
   David O. McKay, CR 10/20:41

The true purpose of life is the perfection of humanity through individual effort, under the guidance of God's inspiration.
   David O. McKay, CR 10/63:7

To be alive only to appetite, pleasure, pride, money-making, and not to goodness and kindness, purity and love, poetry, music, flowers, stars, God and eternal hopes, is to deprive one's self of the real joy of living.
   David O. McKay, CR 10/63:7

The greatest battle of life is fought out within the silent chambers of your own soul.
   David O. McKay, CR 10/54:83, CR 4/69:95

Our lives are made up of small items, of labors performed a little at a time.
   Charles C. Rich, JD 17:170

None of us can be sure that he can finish the course of life in perfect faith and devotion, but all of us can be certain that we can never run the course without starting.
   Stephen L Richards, CR 10/52:102

It doesn't matter very much whether we ride in an oxcart or on an interplanetary missile if our journey is purposeless.
   Sterling W. Sill, CR 4/59:60

The greatest commodity in the universe is life.
  Sterling W. Sill, CR 4/65:87

Isn't it ridiculous that we sometimes live through an entire lifetime and never learn to get up in the morning?
  Sterling W. Sill, CR 10/63:80

We have great concern that our lives may someday come to an end, but the real tragedy is that so many lives never really have a beginning.
  Sterling W. Sill, CR 4/55:118

Life begins when we begin.
  Sterling W. Sill, CR 4/71:37

I am very sure that if we could go today while we walk by faith and stand where we once stood when we walked by sight that we would be willing to crawl on our hands and knees through life for this tremendous opportunity which we presently enjoy.
  Sterling W. Sill, CR 4/75:62

This life is not given to us as a pastime.
  George Albert Smith, CR 10/06:48

It is better to save the life of a man than to raise one from the dead.
  Joseph Smith, HC 5:366

True value in life is not measured in what we have, but in what we do; not in what people think and do for us, but by what we think and do for people.
  Henry D. Taylor, CR 4/62:28

It is far better to die in a good cause than to live in a bad one; it is better to die doing good than to live doing evil.
  Brigham Young, JD 11:134

Life is a way of strenuous duty.
  Levi Edgar Young, CR 10/21:91

Life is too big, too noble, too true for us to stoop to

low things.
Levi Edgar Young, CR 4/13:74

See also: Mortality

LIGHT

There are two ways of spreading light: to be the candle or to be the mirror that reflects it.
Spencer W. Kimball, ACR 8/74:49

From the beginning, people of the world have existed in alternating light and shadows most of the time, with relatively short periods of light.
Spencer W. Kimball, ACR 8/73:74

Light is never found except in the presence of truth.
John A. Widtsoe, CR 4/48:148

LIGHT OF CHRIST

There is a divine spark in every man's soul that never wholly goes out.
Thorpe B. Isaacson, CR 10/56:12, CR 10/65:94

LONELINESS

The basic problem of our time is loneliness—the insecurity and anxiety that come with separation from God, and from one's fellowmen, and from a sense of alienation from self that is almost always present.
Marion D. Hanks, CR 10/70:58

We are never really alone when we love God and accept the friendship of his loving son.
Marion D. Hanks, CR 4/73:164

LOVE

True love is a process. True love requires personal action. Love must be continuing to be real. Love takes time.
Marvin J. Ashton, CR 10/75:160

Love is the only element that can tenderize the human heart.
William R. Bradford, CR 4/76:145

True religion is the activated love of God and of neighbor.
ElRay L. Christiansen, CR 10/61:10

I do not think that any person or any community or any part of the Church of Jesus Christ of Latter-day Saints can go very far astray if they will cultivate the spirit of mercy and charity and love.
Rudger Clawson, CR 4/17:28

Love can overcome many parental mistakes in the raising of their children. But love should not be confused with lack of conviction.
Loren C. Dunn, CR 10/74:12

The test of love is in how we live.
Richard L. Evans, CR 10/69:67

There is nothing in the world that a man should value so highly as the love of those with whom he is associated.
Heber J. Grant, CR 4/32:9

That which is beautiful and good and satisfying to the soul is infinitely more so when shared with those we love.
Marion D. Hanks, CR 10/61:13

Men may write love songs and sing them. They may yearn and hope and dream. But all of this will be only a romantic longing unless there is an exercise of authority that transcends the powers of time and death.
Gordon B. Hinckley, CR 4/74:32

True love is not so much a matter of romance as it is a matter of anxious concern for the well being of one's companion.
Gordon B. Hinckley, CR 4/71:82

We can be judged more by what we love than by what we own.
Thorpe B. Isaacson, CR 10/53:29

Listening is one of the forms of love.
Neal A. Maxwell, ACR 8/72:53

Those who are the best love the best.
Hartman Rector, Jr., CR 10/69:76

The only motive strong enough to induce men to exercise that self-control required by the religion of Jesus is love.
Marion G. Romney, CR 10/62:94

Love alone is an insufficient basis for marriage. Anyone can fall in love with anything. Many people have fallen in love with idleness, profanity, adultery, and drunkeness. Cain fell in love with Satan.
Sterling W. Sill, CR 10/63:81

The deepest expression of spirituality is love.
Robert L. Simpson, CR 10/64:94

A man filled with the love of God is not content with blessing his family alone, but ranges through the whole world, anxious to bless the whole human race.
Joseph Smith, HC 4:227

Love all, but tolerate no iniquity.
N. Eldon Tanner, CR 4/73:123

I learned one thing during my early boyhood, and that is that I cannot hate man and at the same time love God.
Moses Thatcher, CR 4/80:20

We all love that for which we sacrifice.
John H. Vandenberg, CR 4/71:73

We may loathe and hate sin and yet be full of love and charity towards the sinner, just as we may

loathe and despise disease and pain, and at the
same time be full of love and charity towards those
who are afflicted.
Rulon S. Wells, CR 4/14:112

We can measure the degree of love that we
possess for any man or cause, by the sacrifice we
make for him or it.
John A. Widtsoe, CR 4/43:38

See also: Charity, Courtship, Marriage

LOYALTY

Loyalty is a good principle, but never if it means
the surrender of honor.
Alvin R. Dyer, CR 4/65:83

An ounce of loyalty is worth a pound of cleverness.
Franklin D. Richards, CR 4/69:20

The man who in his heart is loyal to the president
of the Church is the man who honors his Deacon,
his Teacher, his Bishop, and his stake officers.
Abraham O. Woodruff, CR 10/03:23

MAN

In the kingdom of our Heavenly Father no man is a
"nobody."
Marvin J. Ashton, CR 4/73:20

Incomprehensibly grand as are the physical
creations of the earth and space, they have been
brought into existence as a means to an end; *they*
are the handiwork of God; *man* is his son.
Hugh B. Brown, CR 10/66:105

The real man is seen and known in the
comparative solitude of the home.
Hugh B. Brown, CR 4/62:88

There is but one real battlefront, and that is with
each individual.
   Victor L. Brown, CR 10/74:150

I believe that all men, as a rule, are more good than
they are bad. I believe there is more good in man
than there is wickedness, more righteousness,
more of the love of truth and charity, justice and
mercy.
   Francis M. Lyman, CR 4/10:33

Men were not created to be damned; but they
were created to be saved.
   Francis M. Lyman, CR 10/98:45

The worth of man is a good measuring rod by
which we may judge of the rightfulness or
wrongfulness of a policy or principle whether in
government, in business or social affairs.
   David O. McKay, CR 10/33:11

The spiritual life is the true life of man.
   David O. McKay, CR 10/56:6

That man is most truly great who is most Christlike.
   David O. McKay, CR 4/51:93

Only in the complete surrender of our inner life
may we rise above the selfish, sordid pull of nature.
   David O. McKay, CR 10/53:10

We find two classes into which all mankind may be
divided—the builders and the murmurers.
   David O. McKay, CR 4/09:63

I believe that there is in every human soul a
something good calling for something better.
   David O. McKay, CR 10/20:43

The only thing which places man above the beasts
of the field is his possession of spiritual gifts.
   David O. McKay, CR 10/51:9

The theory that man is other than the offspring of

God has been, and, so long as it is accepted and acted upon, will continue to be, a major factor in blocking man's spiritual growth and in corrupting his morals.
   Marion G. Romney, CR 4/73:135

The beast was put down on all fours and thus his vision is cast upon the ground, but man was created upright in the image of his maker that he might look up to God.
   Sterling W. Sill, CR 10/75:43

The real worth of a man is not in himself alone, but in what he stands for.
   Sterling W. Sill, CR 4/54:118

That great masterpiece of creation which God fashioned in his own image still remains the mystery of the universe.
   Sterling W. Sill, CR 10/65:55

As man now is, God once was: As God now is, man may be.
   Lorenzo Snow, Improvement Era 22:8 (June 1919), pp. 656, 661

God . . . has bestowed upon us the capacity for infinite wisdom and knowledge, because he has given us a portion of Himself.
   Lorenzo Snow, CR 4/98:63

Man is a dual being, possessed of body and spirit, made in the image of God, and connected with him and with eternity. He is a god in embryo and will live and progress throughout the eternal ages, if obedient to the laws of the Godhead, as the Gods progress throughout the eternal ages.
   John Taylor, JD 23:65

The natural man is of God.
   Brigham Young, JD 9:305

MARRIAGE

Marriage is at all times, in every culture and under the widest of circumstances, one of the supreme tests of human character.
Hugh B. Brown, CR 10/66:104

The time to be married right is when you're married.
ElRay L. Christiansen, CR 4/74:35

There is as much difference between a Temple marriage and a civil marriage as there is between the sun and the moon.
Rudger Clawson, CR 10/37:112

Any man or woman who contracts a Temple marriage in the Church of Jesus Christ of Latter-day Saints and abides by the conditions and restrictions of this great law will have lived a successful life.
Rudger Clawson, CR 10/33:107

Marriage is more than a wedding.
Richard L. Evans, CR 8/71:71

Marriage is the gateway through which a man or woman obtains personal experience in human relationships. Parenthood is the opportunity for putting that experience to heavenly and practical use.
Thorpe B. Isaacson, CR 4/59:64

Young people do not know the true sacredness of marriage until they have been taught by the temple ordinance.
Harold B. Lee, CR 4/57:23

There is no more important single act that any Latter-day Saint ever does in this world than to marry the right person in the right place by the right authority.
Bruce R. McConkie, CR 10/55:13,

Marriage is a state of mutual service.
  David O. McKay, CR 4/69:9

The wedding ring gives no man the right to be
cruel or inconsiderate, and no woman the right to
be slovenly, cross, or disagreeable.
  David O. McKay, CR 4/56:8

During courtship we should keep our eyes wide
open, but after marriage keep them half-shut.
  David O. McKay, CR 4/56:9

The love of husband and wife is an eternal bond,
not sealed lightly in frivolity or passion but entered
into by premeditation, careful observation, sacred
association and prayer.
  David O. McKay, CR 4/30:82

A happy marriage requires constant attention.
  H. Burke Peterson, CR 10/72:149

The difference between civil marriage and celestial
or temple marriage is the difference between
slavery and godhood for eternity.
  Eldred G. Smith, CR 4/50:70

If you don't want a family, don't get married.
  Reed Smoot, CR 4/03:54

  See also: Courtship, Divorce, Family, Love

MARTYRDOM

Living a Christlike life every day may, for many, be
even more difficult than laying down one's life.
  James E. Faust, ACR 8/74:113

That a man is willing to die for his religion is no
proof of its being true; neither is it proof that a
religion is false when one of its votaries apostatizes
from it.
  Brigham Young, JD 7:140

  See also: Death

MEDITATION

Meditation is the language of the soul.
David O. McKay, CR 4/67:85

See also: Prayer, Worship

MEETINGS

I believe it is an offense to God when we leave meetings early, and when we come late to meetings.
Vaughn J. Featherstone, CR 4/75:101

Unless the Saints attend their meetings it will be hard for them to keep alive in the gospel.
Anthon H. Lund, CR 10/07:9

We cannot develop in Godliness without going to the meetings.
Anthon H. Lund, CR 4/20:17

Mere attendance at Church and other acts of piety signify little if the person does not conform his acts and his speech to the principles of the gospel.
David O. McKay, CR 4/61:6

It is the height of rudeness, excepting in an emergency, to leave a worshiping assembly before dismissal.
David O. McKay, CR 10/56:7

No matter how dull or dry the speaking from the pulpit may be, there are still purposes to be subserved in the assembling of the people together that should call the faithful Latter-day Saints to worship.
B. H. Roberts, CR 10/01:35

As president of this house, I forbid any man leaving just as we are going to close the meeting.
Joseph Smith, HC 5:363

See also: Church

MERCY (See Charity, Love)

MILLENNIUM

Men must become harmless, before the brute
creation; and when men lose their vicious
dispositions and cease to destroy the animal race,
the lion and the lamb can dwell together, and the
sucking child can play with the serpent in safety.
Joseph Smith, HC 2:71

I will prophesy that the signs of the coming of the
Son of Man are already commenced.
Joseph Smith, HC 3:390

We are living in the Saturday evening of time. . . .
We are now at the end of the week, in the Saturday
night of human history. Morning will break upon
the Millennium; the thousand years of peace, the
Sabbath of the world.
Orson F. Whitney, CR 10/19:73-74

See also: Latter Days

MIND

The finite mind is not capable of wholly
comprehending the great plan of redemption.
Rudger Clawson, CR 10/04:35

Let us be more concerned about the adornment of
our minds that are eternal, rather than adornment
of our persons with things that are of no lasting
benefit.
George Albert Smith, CR 4/15:97

Thy mind, O man! if thou wilt lead a soul unto
salvation, must stretch as high as the utmost
heavens, and search into and contemplate the
darkest abyss, and the broad expanse of eternity—
thou must commune with God. . . . None but fools
will trifle with the souls of men.
Joseph Smith, HC 3:295

Memory is the library of the mind, in which we find stored away the valuable as well as the worthless things that have come to us. Recollection is the librarian, and he is very often sluggish and sleepy, often neglectful of his duty; he doesn't know where to put his hand on the book or the document we need, just when we need it.
    James E. Talmage, CR 10/13:121

The mind is an attribute of the spirit.
    James E. Talmage, CR 10/22:69

The discipline of the mind is the essence of culture.
    John A. Widtsoe, CR 10/40:64

The greatest mystery a man ever learned, is to know how to control the human mind, and bring every faculty and power of the same in subjection to Jesus Christ; this is the greatest mystery we have to learn while in these tabernacles of clay.
    Brigham Young, JD 1:47

> *See also:* Knowledge

MIRACLE

If a miracle is a supernatural event whose antecedent forces are beyond man's finite wisdom, then the resurrection of Jesus Christ is the most stupendous miracle of all time.
    David O. McKay, CR 4/66:56

We must not expect miracles unless the occasion demands them. God is a wise economist. He would not take a bludgeon to brain a gnat, nor a thunder-bolt to kill a flea. He always suits the weapon to the warfare, the tool to the task required of it.
    Orson F. Whitney, CR 10/19:69

God . . . does not always bring to pass his purposes by means of miracles or through the

instrumentality of his chosen people.
Orson F. Whitney, CR 10/19:69

It might be said that the time will come when miracles will be so common that there will be none.
Orson F. Whitney, CR 4/25:20

They who doubt the possibility of miracles are indeed without the power to perform them.
Orson F. Whitney, CR 4/25:17

Miracles are not contrary to law; they are simply extraordinary results flowing from superior means and methods of doing things.
Orson F. Whitney, CR 10/28:64-65

MISSIONARIES

It is not so important whether a young man has been through the experience of a mission as it is whether the mission experience has been through him.
Marvin J. Ashton, CR 10/74:58

When the devil lays a snare for the feet of a missionary, he generally baits the hook with a woman.
Melvin J. Ballard, CR 4/29:66

The greatest miracle of "Mormonism" today is the miracle of the "Mormon" missionary.
Melvin J. Ballard, CR 4/25:133

We need missionaries to match our message.
Ezra Taft Benson, CR 4/75:96

The missionaries who spend the least money and accept the simple hospitality of the people, accomplish the most work, develop the greatest faith and obtain the greatest results.
Sylvester Q. Cannon, CR 10/38:96

It is not the fact that the Elders are going forth into the world to preach that is so significant, as it is the power and authority which accompanies them.
Rudger Clawson, CR 4/09:93

No missionary has come home with increased light and knowledge to tell us that the gospel is wrong, or that he has discovered the truth in some foreign land.
Heber J. Grant, CR 4/11:21

There is nothing that qualifies a man so much for preaching the gospel of the Lord Jesus Christ as to study the revelations that the Lord has seen fit to give us in our day.
Heber J. Grant, CR 10/25:6

I am confident that the time will never come when we shall not need vigorous men and women of faith to go into the world as missionaries.
Gordon B. Hinckley, CR 4/59:120

It is true that God generally calls upon the illiterate or unlearned to bear his name and testimony to the world. . . . But the question with me is, must the servant of God always remain an unpolished shaft in the quiver of the Almighty? I answer, No.
Orson Hyde, JD 7:68

We are the messengers, and we have the acceptable message.
Spencer W. Kimball, ACR 8/74:141

Every member a missionary.
David O. McKay, CR 4/59:122

The pattern I set in the mission field has been a guide to me throughout my life.
Franklin D. Richards (1821, 1849-1899), CR 10/72:83

Great missionaries have been characterized by their simplicity and their directness.
Franklin D. Richards (1900, 1960-   ), CR 10/62:32

I tell the missionaries that you never need to argue
with anybody when you learn how to tell our story.
  LeGrand Richards, CR 4/73:102

No great message is ever delivered without a great
messenger.
  Sterling W. Sill, CR 10/63:79

The Lord is always looking for men in whom he
can place his full confidence, who can represent
him in the mission field, and men who can be
trusted in every way and who are prepared to help
build his kingdom.
  N. Eldon Tanner, CR 4/75:115

We in fact are the saviours of the world, if they
ever are saved.
  John Taylor, JD 6:163

The men who have had the greatest success in
converting souls to the Church of Jesus Christ of
Latter-day Saints have not been men of very great
learning; they have been men who have been
taught of God, who have been God-fearing,
humble, and willing to give unto Him the honor
and the glory for all they were able to accomplish.
  Abraham O. Woodruff, CR 4/98:19

  See also: Missionary Work

MISSIONARY WORK

Our main task is to declare the gospel and do it
effectively. We are not obligated to answer every
objection. Every man eventually is backed up to
the wall of faith, and there he must make his stand.
  Ezra Taft Benson, CR 4/75:95

The greatest missionary tool we have is that of
demonstrating friendliness, brotherly kindness,
harmony, love and peace in our homes and in all
our church meetings.
  Theodore M. Burton, CR 10/74:77

Considering conditions in the world generally,
there never was a time more cut off from Christ
than ours, or one that needed him more.
Hugh B. Brown, CR 4/65:43

Missionary service is not only a test of *faith* but a
real test of *character.*
ElRay L. Christiansen, CR 4/59:13

Every member of our Church is a missionary.
Without the formality of a setting-apart we should be
so set-apart from the ways of the world that we can
teach the gospel, which is our Father's way of life, by
the very lives we live.
William J. Critchlow, Jr., CR 10/60:28

We will always be a missionary Church.
David B. Haight, CR 10/72:86

There isn't anything else more important than
taking the gospel to the world.
Spencer W. Kimball, ACR 8/71:22

Every LDS male who is worthy and able should fill
a mission.
Spencer W. Kimball, CR 4/74:126

If we overemphasize the philosophies of the
enemies of righteousness instead of teaching
forcefully the principles of the gospel of Jesus
Christ, such overemphasis can only serve to stir up
controversy and strife and thus defeat the very
purpose of our missionary work in all the nations
of the world.
Harold B. Lee, CR 4/72:123

The best means of preaching the gospel is by
personal contact.
David O. McKay, CR 10/69:86

If they put off going upon missions until they can
go without making sacrifices, the time will never
come when they will be prepared to respond to
missionary calls.
Joseph W. McMurrin, CR 4/02:5

There is no power on earth by which we can
penetrate the souls of men, the equal of that
radiation of love and affection which will naturally
pass from us to those to whom we bring truth and
light and knowledge and understanding.
Henry D. Moyle, CR 4/53:127

The service of bringing light to a troubled world
must never end.
L. Tom Perry, CR 10/73:61

God has given a new revelation of himself in
modern times and we are the custodians of the
message.
Mark E. Petersen, CR 4/72:18

We just could not have the Church of Jesus Christ
without the spirit of missionary work.
LeGrand Richards, CR 10/54:57

The first soul that anyone should bring to God is
his own soul.
Sterling W. Sill, CR 4/62:13

Every man holding the priesthood of this Church,
who is magnifying his calling before God, is
preaching the gospel.
David A. Smith, CR 10/21:58

No matter how gifted we may be, or how choice
our language, it is the spirit of our Father that
reaches the heart and brings conviction of the
divinity of this work.
George Albert Smith, CR 10/04:66

We don't ask any people to throw away any good
they have got; we only ask them to come and get
more.
Joseph Smith, HC 5:259

The greatest and most important duty is to preach
the gospel.
Joseph Smith, HC 2:478

Don't let a single corner of the earth go without a mission.
Joseph Smith, HC 5:368

Every man who has a calling to minister to the inhabitants of the world was ordained to that very purpose in the Grand Council of heaven before this world was.
Joseph Smith, HC 6:364

No man can preach the gospel without the Holy Ghost.
Joseph Smith, HC 2:477

Souls are as precious in the sight of God as they ever were.
Joseph Smith, HC 2:229

There is nothing so important, so imperative, as the delivery of the divine message that has been entrusted to us.
Orson F. Whitney, CR 4/15:98

There is no joy that can compare with that of a missionary who has been made the instrument for the salvation of a soul.
Orson F. Whitney, CR 4/18:73

Success in preaching the Gospel springs not from the wisdom of this world.
Brigham Young, JD 8:71

See also: Missionaries

MISTAKES

We are not entitled to any quota of mistakes.
Richard L. Evans, CR 10/69:68

If everyone tried to go back to the beginning to repeat all the mistakes that other men have made, we wouldn't live long enough to learn very much.
Richard L. Evans, CR 4/70:16

Men make mistakes, but God never does.
Francis M. Lyman, CR 4/04:14

When you learn to walk by the Spirit, you never need to make a mistake.
Marion G. Romney, CR 10/61:61

MORALITY

The easiest way to destroy a man's faith is to destroy his morality.
Melvin J. Ballard, CR 4/29:65

Men may succeed, by devious means, in taking property that does not belong to them, but such practices will destroy the moral fiber of their being.
Sylvester Q. Cannon, CR 10/34:87

There is no gain in this world's goods that is worth compromising the life or morals of one young person.
Richard L. Evans, CR 10/70:88

All true morality is supported by and finds its basis in religion.
Stephen L Richards, CR 10/23:47

I was taught that it was more important to be moral than be careful.
George Albert Smith, CR 10/45:50

Reverence for God is the basis of morality.
Levi Edgar Young, CR 4/45:65

See also: Chastity, Virtue

MORMON

The word Mormon, means literally, more good.
Joseph Smith, HC 5:400

MORMONISM

Mormonism is not just a code of ethics; it is not

merely a set of inhibitive injunctions; it is not just a theoretical system of doctrine and philosophy. It is rather a way of life.
Hugh B. Brown, CR 4/56:103

"Mormonism" is a growth. It is not the same today as it was yesterday; for it is growing just like the flower that puts forth its leaves and its buds, and then its blossoms. It is the same plant, but is continually changing, according to conditions and its environment and the necessity to develop itself in its beauty and glory. So also it is in the Church.
Charles W. Penrose, CR 10/05:40

If one is looking for an easy religion, he had better not bother with Mormonism.
LeGrand Richards, CR 4/39:43

I love Mormonism. . . . I love it because its roots run down deep into the great things of God, and it is as a tree well planted, that the winds which beat upon it shall only help by driving its roots deeper into the soil, spreading further to right and left, establishing itself as a tree of God's planting, under whose friendly branches there is room for all who will come unto it; and whose very leaves are sufficient for the healing of the nations.
B. H. Roberts, CR 4/04:19

"Mormonism" does not scatter, does not disintegrate, does not divide; it gathers, unifies, and proposes to bring together all things in Christ.
Orson F. Whitney, CR 4/13:123

Mormonism has in its hand the mightiest weapons that man can wield, divine authority and the power of pure testimony that cuts like a keen two-edged sword.
Orson F. Whitney, CR 4/12:47

Mormonism is no mere nineteenth century religion; it is not merely a religion of time. It is the religion of the eternities, and has come down from the presence of Jehovah, as the preordained plan

for the salvation of the children of men.
Orson F. Whitney, CR 4/08:89

Mormonism is no condemning influence, it is a saving influence for every individual child of the living God.
Levi Edgar Young, CR 10/10:77

"Mormonism" finds its power and efficacy after all in the human heart, it is directed and inspired by the best that is in life and the best that can come from the throne of Almighty God.
Levi Edgar Young, CR 4/13:72

See also: Church

MORTALITY

Mortality is not the ultimate destiny of man.
Albert E. Bowen, CR 4/40:68

Our Heavenly Father . . . didn't send us to earth to be rid of us.
William J. Critchlow, Jr., CR 4/64:30

Man will never be worthy of or capable of appreciating a more glorious state of existence until he has in some measure learned to appreciate the meaning, beauty, and problems of the one in which he now finds himself.
Paul H. Dunn, CR 4/69:148

Don't gamble the peace and happiness and opportunities of eternity against the cheap and shoddy enticements of time.
Richard L. Evans, CR 4/70:16

Some can see the greatness of the past, some can sense the potential of the future, but few are able to recognize the greatness of the present.
John Longden, CR 4/66:39

If we want to be great souls in heaven, we should

practice being great souls here.
  Sterling W. Sill, CR 10/62:39

The Savior is even more concerned for our success
here in mortality than we ourselves are.
  Robert L. Simpson, CR 4/73:17

Today is the beginning of eternal happiness or
eternal disappointment for you.
  George Albert Smith, CR 10/44:94

The God of heaven, our Father, never planted a
single individual upon the earth without a purpose
and design.
  Daniel H. Wells, JD 19:86

The present is the outcome of the past; and it is the
great hook upon which the future hangs.
  Orson F. Whitney, CR 4/16:64

No man can rise very high who lives by earthly
things alone.
  John A. Widtsoe, CR 4/40:38

It is the business of man to find the spiritual
meaning of earthly things.
  John A. Widtsoe, CR 4/22:96

  See also: Adversity, Birth, Death, Life, Time

MOTHER

Fathers have heads, but mothers have hearts; and
hearts will know things that heads never can
understand.
  Boyd K. Packer, ACR 8/71:127

Do without if you need to, but don't do without
mother.
  H. Burke Peterson, CR 4/74:44

Whenever we have great men, the mother's
influence generally had more to do than anything
else with their accomplishment and success.
  N. Eldon Tanner, ACR 8/72:93

It is the mothers, after all, that rule the nations of the earth. They form, dictate, and direct the minds of statesmen, and the feelings, course, life, notions, and sentiments of the great and the small, of kings, rulers, governors, and of the people in general.
Brigham Young, JD 9:38

If a mother wishes to control her child, in the first place let her learn to control herself, then she may be successful in bringing the child into perfect subjection to her will.
Brigham Young, JD 14:277

See also: Motherhood, Wife, Working Mother

MOTHERHOOD

God, choosing woman to be his partner in the creative process, tucked away somewhere in her bosom a spark of his divine love, which later, at the time of motherhood, glows to brilliancy in every mother's heart.
William J. Critchlow, Jr., CR 10/65:38

Motherhood is the greatest vocation.
Spencer W. Kimball, CR 4/75:8

A successful mother is one who is never too tired for her sons and daughters to come and share their joys and their sorrows with her.
Harold B. Lee, ACR 8/72:91

The greatest responsibility given to women is the divine gift to be a mother.
David O. McKay, CR 10/48:119

See also: Mother

MOTIVES

Motives may be regarded as constituting an index to the character of the individual.
James E. Talmage, CR 4/32:100

I would rather a man do a good deed even with a motive that may not be the best than that he should fail to do it; and far rather that he should do that good deed rather than do evil.
James E. Talmage, CR 4/32:100

See also: Desire, Intentions

MUSIC

We get nearer to the Lord through music than perhaps through any other thing except prayer.
J. Reuben Clark, Jr., CR 10/36:111

If you will show me the songs which a people or a community sing, then I will tell you the character of that community.
Rudger Clawson, CR 4/07:32

The most effective preaching of the gospel is when it is accompanied by beautiful appropriate music.
Harold B. Lee, CR 4/73:181

Good music is gracious praise of God.
Joseph F. Smith, CR 10/99:69

NATIONALISM

There is no other way that all men can be united in a cause that is greater than their own nationalism, except in the acceptance of the universal gospel of Jesus Christ.
A. Theodore Tuttle, CR 4/62:122

See also: Governments, Politics

NATURE

If nature were to violate law as men do, we could not be assured a succession of the seasons, nor a harvest, nor daily sustenance, nor any order of events.
Richard L. Evans, CR 10/65:43

Self-preservation is the first great law of nature.
Heber C. Kimball, JD 11:208

Only in the complete surrender of our inner life
may we rise above the selfish, sordid pull of nature.
David O. McKay, CR 10/53:10

There is a close connection between the
righteousness or sinfulness of mankind and the
occurrence of natural phenomena.
James E. Talmage, CR 10/23:49

See also: Instinct

NEGLECT

Be determined that no boy or girl is going to be
lost because of your neglect.
N. Eldon Tanner, CR 10/74:110

OBEDIENCE

Any Church member not obedient to the leaders of
this Church will not have the opportunity to be
obedient to the promptings of the Lord.
Marvin J. Ashton, ACR 8/73:23

Had any man accepted the ancient scripture in the
days of Noah but refused to follow the revelation
that Noah received and failed to board the ark, he
would have been drowned.
Ezra Taft Benson, CR 10/72:54

The observance of divine instructions is the most
effective means for the best development of men
and women.
Sylvester Q. Cannon, CR 10/29:44

The greatest work we can do is to so live that we
ourselves shall be saved, that our own acts shall be
correct, and our will and desires and passions be
brought into subjection to the will of God.
George Q. Cannon, JD 20:291

Mere obedience in spiritual matters requires that on occasion it shall be blind obedience because the Lord cannot explain to us all the things that he asks us to do. We could not understand.
J. Reuben Clark, Jr., CR 10/53:39

Obedience must often precede knowledge.
J. Reuben Clark, Jr., CR 4/50:181

The great success which attended the ministry of Jesus Christ was due to His strict obedience to the will of the Father.
Rudger Clawson, CR 10/02:51

✻ We ought to keep the commandments simply as a favor to ourselves.
Richard L. Evans, CR 10/71:33

It is the specific performance of specific things that makes men better—not theory, not merely the fact that there is a set of principles or that there are commandments, or that there is counsel, but the living of it.
Richard L. Evans, CR 10/58:60

The price of discipleship is obedience.
James E. Faust, ACR 8/74:112

No obstacles are insurmountable when God commands and we obey.
Heber J. Grant, CR 10/99:18

The seeing of an angel amounts to nothing, unless you are keeping the commandments of God.
Heber J. Grant, CR 10/00:34

Obedience is the first law of God.
Francis M. Lyman, CR 10/99:35

There is an inseparable connection between the keeping of the commandments and the well-being of society.
Neal A. Maxwell, CR 10/74:15

Every world problem may be solved by obedience
to the principles of the gospel of Jesus Christ.
David O. McKay, CR 4/20:116

It won't be the things that we don't know that will
give us trouble. It will be the things that we do
know and fail to abide by.
Thomas E. McKay, CR 10/48:67

The price we pay by lending obedience to the laws
of the gospel sinks into insignificance when
compared with our incomparable receipts.
Henry D. Moyle, CR 10/62:89

In the kingdom of God the path of obedience is
not only the path of safety, but it is the path of
salvation.
George Reynolds, CR 10/01:44

Obedience is not only the first law of heaven, but
obedience is the fundamental requirement of all
good government.
Stephen L Richards, CR 4/20:98

The most challenging, dramatic, and vital thing in
our lives is this "keeping the commandments." It
tests every fiber of our beings. It is at once a
demonstration of our intelligence, our knowledge,
our character, and our wisdom.
Stephen L Richards, CR 4/49:138

Obedience to the commandments here referred
to—the principles and ordinances of the gospel—
constitutes the sure and only means of escaping the
impending calamity.
Marion G. Romney, CR 10/58:97

We are no better than the rest of the world, except
to the degree to which we accept the
commandments of the Lord and obey them.
Marion G. Romney, CR 10/46:74

There can be no equal to the peace of mind that
always comes as the reward for obedience to truth.
Robert L. Simpson, CR 10/67:19

We have no new commandment to give, but admonish Elders and members to live by every word that proceedeth forth from the mouth of God.
Joseph Smith, HC 5:404

I made this my rule: *When the Lord commands, do it.*
Joseph Smith, HC 2:170

We cannot keep all the commandments without first knowing them, and we cannot expect to know all, or more than we now know unless we comply with or keep those we have already received.
Joseph Smith, HC 5:135

There can be no true, perfect civilization where there is not faithful obedience to the commandments of God.
Joseph Fielding Smith, CR 4/35:96

God's work and His Church will grow and increase just as fast as we, the members of it, are capable of carrying out the instructions of God.
Reed Smoot, CR 4/15:93

Obedience is not blind when it is based on faith.
Henry D. Taylor, CR 4/66:82

There is no aristocracy in heaven except as we obey or disobey the commandments of God.
John A. Widtsoe, CR 4/50:129

We all have to be obedient to someone.
Abraham O. Woodruff, CR 4/01:12

Having a principle explained is one thing, teaching its application is another thing, but getting obedience to it is a third thing.
S. Dilworth Young, CR 4/52:29

See also: Righteousness

OLD AGE

A civilization is marked by its attitude toward the aged.
    Marvin O. Ashton, CR 10/44:105

Some say they are too old to improve, but there is no person too old to be damned for their sins.
    Heber C. Kimball, JD 9:328

We have a wonderful age retirement plan in this Church. . . . We grow younger in this Church as we work in it, and the age retirement plan goes in reverse. The older we get and the longer we labor in the Church the more there is that we can do.
    George Q. Morris, CR 4/52:31

OPPOSITION (See Adversity, Satan, Sin, Trial)

OPTIMISM

The spirit of the gospel is optimistic; it trusts in God and looks on the bright side of things. The opposite or pessimistic spirit drags men down and away from God, looks on the dark side, murmurs, complains, and is slow to yield obedience.
    Orson F. Whitney, CR 4/17:43

PARENTHOOD

Marriage is the gateway through which a man or woman obtains personal experience in human relationships. Parenthood is the opportunity for putting that experience to heavenly and practical use.
    Thorpe B. Isaacson, CR 4/59:64

Pure water does not flow from a polluted spring—nor a healthy nation from a diseased parentage.
    David O. McKay, CR 4/43:20

There is something in the depths of the human soul

which revolts against neglectful parenthood.
David O. McKay, CR 4/35:112

See also: Children, Family, Parents

PARENTS

Parents who indulge themselves "in moderation" may have children who indulge themselves to excess.
Richard L. Evans, CR 4/69:75

Parents are deceiving themselves in imagining that their children will be born with a knowledge of the gospel.
Heber J. Grant, CR 4/02:80

If our society is coming apart at the seams, it is because the tailor and the seamstress in the home are not producing the kind of stitching that will hold under stress.
Gordon B. Hinckley, CR 10/68:56

Good citizens are necessary to civilization, but good parents are obligatory if civilization is to continue.
Thorpe B. Isaacson, CR 4/59:64

Parent love is beautiful, but parent love combined with intelligent discipline is the force that turns children into great characters.
Thorpe B. Isaacson, CR 4/59:64

Most ills of life are due to failure of parents to teach their children and the failure of posterity to listen.
Spencer W. Kimball, ACR 8/74:48

I believe it is generally understood, and advocated, that if we were better parents, better fathers and mothers, attended more faithfully to our duties in teaching our children and training them, we would have better children.
Francis M. Lyman, CR 4/09:119-20

Parents who do not know where their children are at night are recreant to the sacred obligation of

parenthood and untrue to the high ideals of the
Church regarding home life.
  David O. McKay, CR 10/51:10

Parents in Zion will be held responsible for the acts of
their children, not only until they become eight years
old but, perhaps, throughout all the lives of their
children, provided they have neglected their duty to
their children while they were under their care and
guidance, and the parents were responsible for them.
  Joseph F. Smith, CR 4/10:6

The parents that you should honor more than any
others are the parents of your children-to-be.
  N. Eldon Tanner, ACR 8/71:71

Parents must realize that every word they speak, every
act, every response, attitude, and even appearance
and manner of dress will affect the lives of their
children and the whole family.
  N. Eldon Tanner, ACR 8/74:63

You should never say a word or do an act which you
would not want your children to copy after.
  John Taylor, JD 26:112

Stable, secure, well-balanced individuals are not
accidental. They are the result of prayerful,
concentrated attention to parental responsibilities.
  A. Theodore Tuttle, CR 4/67:94

Only out of purposeful, divine relationship of parent
and child grows eternal joy and fulfillment.
  A. Theodore Tuttle, CR 10/72:70

  See also: Children, Family, Husband, Parenthood, Wife

PASSIONS

The "natural man" is the "earthy man" who has
allowed rude animal passions to overshadow his
spiritual inclinations.
  Spencer W. Kimball, CR 10/74:161

You show me a man who has complete control over his appetite, who can resist all temptations to indulge in stimulants, liquor, tobacco, marijuana, and other vicious drugs, and I will show you a youth or man who has likewise developed power to control his passions and desires.
   David O. McKay, CR 4/68:8

Our passions are good, and planted within us for a good and wise purpose, to give us strength and energy of character; but they should be governed and controlled by that heaven-inspired intellect and reason with which every person is endowed.
   Daniel H. Wells, JD 15:88

   See also: Appetite, Emotion, Temptation

PATIENCE

There is a point at which patience ceases to be a virtue, and then it will become necessary to act, or advise at least.
   Joseph F. Smith, CR 4/13:7

PATRIOTISM

Wherever you live be patriotic to the country in which you live; not only to the soil and to the elements, by which God shall sustain your lives while you promote his work in that land, but be patriotic to the institutions of the country; under whose flag you receive your rights and have the opportunity to life, liberty and the pursuit of happiness.
   Matthias F. Cowley, CR 10/01:19

   See also: Governments, Nationalism

PEACE

We never get stomach ulcers because of what we eat; we get stomach ulcers because of what is eating us.
   Anon. Sterling W. Sill, CR 4/72:156

The most severe test that has ever come to any people is the test of peace and prosperity.
Melvin J. Ballard, CR 10/28:110

There can be no peace in a Godless world.
Hugh B. Brown, CR 10/60:94

Peace cannot come by legislation or through affiliation with any political philosophy. . . . Peace, joy, and happiness can come only through an acceptance of God's revealed plan of life.
Theodore M. Burton, CR 10/71:75

The longer we are members of the Church, the better we understand the gospel, the more we will be inclined to be peacefully minded. The more diligently we follow the teaching of Christ, the slower we will be to be angry with each other and the quicker we will be to forgive each other.
Theodore M. Burton, ACR 8/73:98

Peace is more than a spot of ink on a piece of paper or a sound upon our lips. It is the application of the teachings of the Prince of Peace in our daily lives.
John Longden, CR 10/64:126

Do what you can to produce peace and harmony, no matter what you may suffer.
David O. McKay, CR 4/63:130

Peace springs from righteousness in the soul, from upright living.
David O. McKay, CR 10/53:133

No man is at peace with himself or his God who is untrue to his better self, who transgresses the law of right either in dealing with himself by indulging in passion, in appetite, yielding to temptations against his accusing conscience, or in dealing with his fellowmen, being untrue to their trust.
David O. McKay, CR 10/38:133

There is no happiness without peace.
David O. McKay, CR 10/53:132

There is no road to universal peace, which does not lead to the heart of humanity.
  David O. McKay, CR 10/44:81

Peace, when it comes to the world, will be made up of the many tricklets of love flowing from the hearts of the people to a common understanding and a common goal.
  Thomas E. McKay, CR 10/45:80

The measure of peace that we have or shall have will be proportionate to the degree of fullness to which the aggressor observes the golden rule.
  Joseph F. Merrill, CR 4/50:58

Peace will replace fear in men's hearts when they listen to the counsel of God's prophet and accept and follow the principles of the restored gospel of Jesus Christ.
  Franklin D. Richards (1900, 1960-   ), CR 4/66:140

Dear as peace is to me, it is not so dear that I would purchase it at the sacrifice of human rights and human liberty.
  B. H. Roberts, CR 10/12:34

Peace among men and nations will be the natural sequence when enough individuals have peace in their hearts.
  Marion G. Romney, CR 4/70:67

It is not because we do not know the remedy that peace escapes us. It is because we do not know the God to whom we must return.
  Marion G. Romney, CR 4/70:67

The only real peace in this world is peace of mind.
  Robert L. Simpson, CR 10/70:101

There can be no equal to the peace of mind that always comes as the reward for obedience to truth.
  Robert L. Simpson, CR 10/67:19

We carry to the world the olive branch of peace.
  Joseph F. Smith, CR 4/02:2

Our mission to the world is a mission of peace.
John Taylor, JD 23:263-64

Peace is rooted in righteousness! It grows not in the soil of sin or in indifference to the spirit of God. It occurs not by edict of force. It comes by voluntary change in the heart of man.
A. Theodore Tuttle, CR 10/62:97

Peace cannot be achieved by making a sign or by writing words on fences. It must come first and most completely to the individual through his own efforts in keeping the commandments of our Lord and Savior.
John H. Vandenberg, CR 4/72:161

There will be no peace on earth, no final solution of man's vexing problems, until leaders and followers humble themselves to receive guidance from the heavens.
John A. Widtsoe, CR 10/34:11

A man never finds perfect peace, never reaches afar unless he penetrates to some degree the unseen world, and reaches out to touch the hands, as it were, of those who live in that unseen world, the world out of which we came, the world into which we shall go.
John A. Widtsoe, CR 10/38:129

If I pick an apple from a tree, I have first planted the tree, cared for it, watered it, brought it to maturity. Then in due time I may have the fruit. So with peace. It is not a thing by itself to be picked up casually; but it is the fruit of something precedent.
John A. Widtsoe, CR 10/46:12-13

No lasting peace can come to this world until a *peace* is based on the love of God for all peoples.
Levi Edgar Young, CR 10/20:173

PERCEPTION

The limit of our spiritual perception is the horizon we see.
Joseph Anderson, CR 4/72:88

If we attend solely to observation and the summing up of evil alone, we are very apt to get a mis-vision of things.
B. H. Roberts, CR 4/22:99

PERFECTION

The whole purpose and object of life is to achieve individual perfection through the unfolding of individual potentialities and the ripening of all the virtues.
Albert E. Bowen, CR 4/38:9

The more perfect one becomes, the less he is inclined to speak of the imperfections of others.
ElRay L. Christiansen, CR 4/56:114

There is no man in the Church of Christ who claims infallibility.
Heber J. Grant, CR 10/07:25

I accept Jesus Christ as the personification of human perfection.
David O. McKay, CR 10/65:144

Perfection cannot come by imperfect means.
Mark E. Petersen, CR 10/74:67

The Gospel . . . is God's own guide to a perfect life.
George F. Richards, CR 10/06:67

Things that men do will never be perfect until they themselves reach the perfection of Christ, the perfect one.
Stephen L Richards, CR 10/38:116

No man can become perfect in Christ without a deep, abiding, and sincere concern for his fellow beings.
Robert L. Simpson, CR 4/73:19

Perfection in one thing will act as a stepping-stone to perfection in something else, and soon we may approach perfection in all things.
Sterling W. Sill, CR 10/62:38

The nearer man approaches perfection, the clearer are his views, and the greater his enjoyments, till he has overcome the evils of his life and lost every desire for sin.
Joseph Smith, HC 2:8

Perfection dwells not with mortal man.
Joseph F. Smith, CR 4/06:7

Perfection is rather relative than absolute.
James E. Talmage, CR 4/15:123

We are not required in our sphere to be as perfect as Gods and angels are in their spheres, yet man is the king of kings and lord of lords in embryo.
Brigham Young, JD 10:223

PERSECUTION

Always remember that the Lord is stronger than those who oppose Him.
Anthon H. Lund, CR 4/05:15

The Church is little if at all injured by persecution and calumnies from ignorant, misinformed or malicious enemies; a great hindrance to its progress comes from fault-finders, shirkers, commandment-breakers, and apostate cliques within its own ecclesiastical and quorum groups.
David O. McKay, CR 10/39:103

From apostates the faithful have received the severest persecutions.
Joseph Smith, HC 2:23

Hell may pour forth its rage like the burning lava of Mount Vesuvius, or of Etna, or of the most terrible of the burning mountains; and yet shall "Mormonism" stand.
Joseph Smith, HC 3:297

Those who cannot endure persecution, and stand in the day of affliction, cannot stand in the day when the Son of God shall burst the veil, and appear in all the

glory of His Father, with all the holy angels.
  Joseph Smith, HC 1:468

Persecutions may rage, mobs may combine, armies
may assemble, calumny may defame, but the truth of
God will go forth boldly, nobly, and independent, till
it has penetrated every continent, visited every clime,
swept every country, and sounded in every ear, till the
purposes of God shall be accomplished, and the great
Jehovah shall say the work is done.
  Joseph Smith, HC 4:540

A persecuted religion will be an investigated religion.
  Moses Thatcher, JD 25:115

When they blow out the sun and stop the moon from
shining and the earth from revolving on its axis, they
may talk about "wiping out" the "Mormons" or the
Gospel, but not until then.
  Brigham Young, JD 13:94

  See also: Church

PERSEVERANCE

Footprints in the sands of time are not made by sitting
down.
  Anon. Carl W. Buehner, CR 4/55:62

What's the use of running when you're on the wrong
road?
  Anon. Richard L. Evans, CR 4/68:87

History rests on the shoulders of those who accepted
the challenge of difficulties and drove through to
victory in spite of everything.
  Hugh B. Brown, CR 10/63:87

The summer patriot and the sunshine Saint retreat
when the battle wages fiercely around them. Theirs is
not the conqueror's crown. They are overcome by the
world.
  Bruce R. McConkie, CR 10/74:45

  See also: Endurance

PHILOSOPHY

Philosophy and theology may be interesting and give us lofty concepts, and we may become inspired by profound thinking, but Christian faith is based upon the simplicity of the gospel, the example, the life, and the teachings of Jesus Christ.
Howard W. Hunter, CR 4/69:138

We are not called to preach the philosophies of men mingled with scripture.
Hartman Rector, Jr., CR 10/73:133

There is no science, nor philosophy that can supersede God Almighty's truth.
Joseph F. Smith, CR 4/11:7

Any doctrine, whether it comes in the name of religion, science, philosophy, or whatever it may be, if it is in conflict with the revealed word of the Lord, will fail.
Joseph Fielding Smith, CR 10/52:60

There is a philosophy of the earth and a philosophy of the heavens; the latter can unravel all mysteries pertaining to earth; but the philosophy of the earth cannot enter into the mysteries of the kingdom of God, or the purposes of the Most High.
John Taylor, JD 13:222

PLANNING

If we start right, it is easy to go right all the time; but if we start wrong we may go wrong, and it will be a hard matter to get right.
Joseph Smith, HC 6:303

PLEASURE

Those who pursue pleasure in this life to excess are likely to forsake the ways of the Lord.
George Albert Smith, CR 4/15:95

There is no lasting pleasure here, unless it is in God.
Brigham Young, JD 18:213

POLITICS

Our religion should purify our politics, and make us honest, tolerant, and bold, to do that which is required of citizens, and to exercise our rights at the polls.
James E. Talmage, CR 10/20:66-67

See also: Governments, Nationalism

POPULARITY

Seldom are men willing to oppose a popular program if they themselves wish to be popular.
Ezra Taft Benson, CR 10/68:17

That which is right does not become wrong merely because it may be deserted by the majority, neither does that which is wrong today become right tomorrow by the chance circumstance that it has won the approval or been adopted by overwhelmingly predominant numbers.
Albert E. Bowen, CR 4/41:85

It is not the numerical strength that constitutes the power and strength of a people; it is their purity of life, and their possession of the Holy Spirit as a source of inspiration in all the walks of life.
Matthias F. Cowley, CR 10/01:16

An idiotic opinion multiplied by fifty million is still an idiotic opinion.
Richard L. Evans, CR 10/48:63

We will not be popular with those who are unrighteous.
George Albert Smith, CR 10/21:161

That a thing is popular is frequently justification for the Latter-day Saints to avoid it.
George Albert Smith, CR 4/33:71

It is our duty to concentrate all our influence to make popular that which is sound and good, and unpopular that which is unsound.
Joseph Smith, HC 5:286

PORNOGRAPHY

Pornography . . . is really garbage, but today is peddled as normal and satisfactory food.
Spencer W. Kimball, CR 10/74:7

POTENTIAL

The greatest loss . . . is the loss that results from the failure of individuals to reach their potential.
William H. Bennett, CR 4/74:46

When a man is convinced that he is truly a son of God or a woman is convinced that she is truly a daughter of God, there are no limits to the growth of that person.
Theodore M. Burton, CR 10/71:76

Compared with what we might be, we are only half alive.
Sterling W. Sill, CR 10/62:39

See also: Success

POVERTY

If we neglect the poor, God will neglect us.
Rudger Clawson, CR 4/99:5

We may be faced with a lowered physical standard of living, but we need not be faced with lowered standards of thinking.
Richard L. Evans, CR 4/52:67

If you struggle financially, but have all the blessings of heaven, you are rich indeed.
Spencer W. Kimball, ACR 8/74:102

POWER

Purity is power.
Hugh B. Brown, CR 4/64:56

With every gift of power comes the temptation to abuse it.
Hugh B. Brown, CR 4/64:55

All beings who have bodies have power over those who have not.
Joseph Smith, Compendium, p. 271

In knowledge there is power. God has more power than all other beings, because he has greater knowledge; and hence he knows how to subject all other beings to him. He has power over all.
Joseph Smith, HC 5:340

Unity is power.
Joseph Smith, HC 6:198

See also: Priesthood

PRAISE

I would rather have a single flower given to me in life by a friend than I would have my coffin banked with roses.
Reed Smoot, CR 10/07:59

PRAYER

From simple trials to our Gethsemanes, prayer can put us in touch with God, our greatest source of comfort and counsel.
Ezra Taft Benson, CR 10/74:91

There is not anything that this world needs more than for all of our people, young and old, to be on their knees, night and morning, recognizing the need for divine guidance and divine support.
Ezra Taft Benson, ACR 8/74:70

Unbelief . . . has a tendency to prevent the communication of God's will to man by closing the channel of communication.
George Q. Cannon, JD 14:170

Prayer must have as a foundation, repentance of sin and faith.
J. Reuben Clark, Jr., CR 10/52:42

Prayer is the royal road between each of us and our Heavenly Father. Whether it remains open or is closed is for our determination.
J. Reuben Clark, Jr., CR 10/58:45

No men are greater than when they are upon their knees in communion with God.
Matthew Cowley, CR 10/53:109

You show me a man who is constantly engaged in prayer and supplication, and I will point to you a man that does not have to be preached to.
Matthias F. Cowley, CR 10/00:20

My father prayed; he didn't say his prayers.
Alonzo A. Hinckley, CR 10/34:53

While paying attention to the prayers of some persons in their family devotions, I sometimes notice that they often stop praying without breaking through the darkness and obtaining the Holy Spirit.
Jedediah M. Grant, JD 4:151

Our prayers in private and family circle are secret and retired from the public, but they keep the fire burning upon the altar of our hearts.
Orson Hyde, JD 19:57

Prayer is . . . the gateway through which the repentant sinner may find his way back to God.
Anthony W. Ivins, CR 10/22:91

None of us should get so busy that we crowd out contemplation and praying.
Spencer W. Kimball, CR 4/76:71

Prayer is the passport to spiritual power.
Spencer W. Kimball, CR 4/73:153

Prayer, like radium, is a source of luminous, self-generating energy.
Richard R. Lyman, CR 4/41:68

A praying man is a growing man.
David O. McKay, CR 4/29:101

Prayer is a remedy for divorce.
Thomas E. McKay, CR 4/49:33

Our glimpse of Gethsemane should teach us that all prayers are petitions.
Neal A. Maxwell, CR 4/76:40

Often our prayers are not answered at the very moment we ask them, but at later times.
Boyd K. Packer, ACR 8/74:19

Prayer alone is but lip service.
Mark E. Petersen, CR 4/68:62

The Church of Jesus Christ of Latter-day Saints is truly a monument to prayer.
Franklin D. Richards (1900, 1960-   ), CR 4/72:66

The laws governing prayer are as immutable as those governing science.
Franklin D. Richards (1900, 1960-   ), CR 4/72:69

The path from man to God is prayer.
Marion G. Romney, CR 10/61:61

Prayer is the catalyst with which we open the door to the Savior.
Marion G. Romney, CR 4/73:118

Prayer is the means by which men communicate with God. Revelation is the means by which God communicates with men.
Marion G. Romney, CR 4/64:122

It is not always the words we use in prayer that count

so much as the spirit in which they are said.
Eldred G. Smith, CR 4/55:41

Praying without humility is praying without faith.
Eldred G. Smith, CR 4/55:41

The Lord can hear a simple prayer, offered in faith, in half a dozen words, and he will recognize fasting that may not continue more than twenty-four hours, just as readily and as effectually as he will answer a prayer of a thousand words and fasting for a month.
Joseph F. Smith, CR 10/12:134

Our prayers are not for the purpose of telling [the Lord] how to run his business.
Joseph Fielding Smith, CR 4/68:10

No man can retain the Spirit of the Lord, unless he prays. No man can have the inspiration of the Holy Spirit, unless in his heart is found this spirit of prayer.
Joseph Fielding Smith, CR 10/19:142

Prayer is the proper way of communication between God's children and himself; when that communication ceases, then spiritual decay begins.
Reed Smoot, CR 10/08:76

Prayer is the Lord's great sterilizer against the germs of spiritual disease.
James E. Talmage, CR 10/21:188

The prayer of the heart is greater than the prayer of the lips.
James E. Talmage, CR 10/31:50

Those who think that they can succeed without praying, try it, and I will promise them eternal destruction, if they persist in that course.
Brigham Young, JD 7:205

PREMORTAL EXISTENCE

When you do take the wrong course, you are undoing

the work of your prior existence.
  ElRay L. Christiansen, CR 4/74:35

We believe that we are harvesting the fruits of our preexistent lives and earning here the reward we expect to reap when we go hence.
  George Albert Smith, CR 4/07:18

Every man who has a calling to minister to the inhabitants of the world was ordained to that very purpose in the Grand Council of heaven before this world was.
  Joseph Smith, HC 6:364

The contention in heaven was—Jesus said there would be certain souls that would not be saved; and the devil said he would save them all.
  Joseph Smith, HC 6:314

  See also: Intelligences

PREACHING

We cannot save those who are indifferent and careless by preaching to them. We must go into their homes.
  David A. Smith, CR 4/33:31

There is no work that any of us can engage in that is as important as preaching the gospel and building up the Church and kingdom of God on earth.
  Joseph Fielding Smith, CR 4/72:13

  See also: Speaking

PREPAREDNESS

There is no situation that has arisen since the organization of this Church, neither will there be, in the future, that the Lord has not made ample provision to meet.
  Melvin J. Ballard, CR 10/27:63

The Lord will inspire His servants and His people so

that they will not be found unprepared.
  George Q. Cannon, CR 4/98:9

Whatever may come here or hereafter, the future will always be better for those who are best prepared.
  Richard L. Evans, CR 4/50:105

Many elements of truth come only after a lifetime of preparation.
  Boyd K. Packer, CR 4/74:138

It wasn't raining when Noah built the ark!
  A. Theodore Tuttle, CR 4/70:86

  See also: Food Storage

PRIDE

An egotist will never get anywhere in this world because he thinks he's already there.
  Marvin J. Ashton, CR 10/74:57

The proud and the haughty are only they who compare themselves with more unfortunate people than they.
  Antoine R. Ivins, CR 10/43:110

No man can compare himself with his ideals and be proud and haughty.
  Antoine R. Ivins, CR 10/43:110

As soon as you think you can lick the devil alone, on your own, without the Lord's help, you have lost the battle.
  Eldred G. Smith, CR 10/71:15

When men get what is called the "big head," it is because there is nothing in their heads.
  John Taylor, JD 11:75

PRIESTHOOD

⚹ We may have the priesthood without the Church, but

never the Church without the priesthood.
Ezra Taft Benson, CR 10/48:99

You cannot show reverence to the priesthood without showing it to to the men who bear it.
George Q. Cannon, CR 4/00:14

Faith is the implementing force of the priesthood.
J. Reuben Clark, Jr., CR 4/53:54

There is no appointment in this Church, that I know of, that is absolutely permanent, excepting the holy priesthood, which we are called to hold.
Rudger Clawson, CR 10/01:65

We have a great body of Priesthood in the Church. . . . These men have been organized into quorums and are being disciplined for war.
Rudger Clawson, CR 4/15:87

Even the angels of heaven respect the Priesthood of God upon the earth.
Matthias F. Cowley, CR 10/01:18

Carelessness around electric power lines can be suddenly lethal. Carelessness around priesthood power lines can be slowly lethal, producing a lingering, withering, spiritual death.
William J. Critchlow, Jr., CR 4/64:31

✦ Priesthood is God's greatest gift to his children, save perhaps the gift of his Son, our Lord and Savior Jesus Christ.
William J. Critchlow, Jr., CR 10/63:29

I do not speak *by* authority or *from* authority, but *with* authority.
Marion D. Hanks, CR 4/71:131

To love the Lord and our fellowmen is the key by which we unlock the power of the priesthood.
Howard W. Hunter, ACR 8/71:98

The power of the Church is in the administration of the priesthood offices.
Antoine R. Ivins, CR 10/60:106

It is impossible to honor the priesthood and not honor the vessel that holds it.
Heber C. Kimball, JD 11:80

The Lord never intended His organized priesthood to fall in behind the auxiliary organizations of the Church.
J. Golden Kimball, CR 10/01:32

The priesthood of God is the most serious thing in the world.
Spencer W. Kimball, ACR 8/74:100

Every presiding position [one holds] will have a bearing on what one is called to do when he leaves this earth.
Harold B. Lee, CR 10/72:130

The term "Elder" which is applied to all holders of the Melchizedek Priesthood, means a defender of the faith.
Harold B. Lee, CR 4/70:54

No man in this Church is entitled to receive divine authority from the Lord, and then forget him.
Francis M. Lyman, CR 10/11:35

If priesthood meant only personal distinction or individual elevation, there would be no need of groups or quorums.
David O. McKay, CR 10/62:119, CR 10/68:84

When a man accepts the Priesthood, he accepts the obligation of controlling himself under any circumstances.
David O. McKay, CR 10/58:87

There is a link between every man ordained to the Priesthood and his God.
Charles W. Penrose, CR 10/21:20

This priesthood is a reality and not a mere name; it is not a mere calling in word, but an office which confers upon us power and influence that comes from the

Almighty.
Charles W. Penrose, JD 21:49

Every man who has been called to hold the Priesthood should endeavor to qualify himself for the work that lies before him, both that which he will be called to do while he dwells in the body, and that which he will have to perform when he goes out of the body.
Charles W. Penrose, CR 4/06:86

Our success in the priesthood depends on the pattern of our life.
H. Burke Peterson, CR 10/74:99

Priesthood bearers who are out of harmony with their priesthood leaders are out of harmony with the Lord and are not magnifying their priesthood callings.
Marion G. Romney, ACR 8/72:74

God will not countenance an unclean priesthood.
Marion G. Romney, CR 4/74:117

The safest way to avoid being led astray is to magnify our priesthood.
Marion G. Romney, CR 10/60:78

Seclusion is incompatible with the spirit of the priesthood.
Robert L. Simpson, CR 4/62:78

Every man holding the priesthood of this Church, who is magnifying his calling before God, is preaching the gospel.
David A. Smith, CR 10/21:58

No man is worthy of the priesthood unless he knows what its duties are, and unless he is willing to work with all his might under that responsibility.
David A. Smith, CR 10/19:137

There is no such thing as priesthood power that enables a man to elevate or benefit himself, except as he serves others.
Eldred G. Smith, CR 4/67:77-78

You cannot show disrespect to the priesthood without bringing upon yourselves the displeasure of the Lord.
Hyrum M. Smith, CR 10/11:42

All men who hold the holy priesthood are authorities in the Church.
Hyrum M. Smith, CR 10/05:22

A learned Priesthood is certainly more honorable than "an hireling clergy."
Joseph Smith, HC 6:206

Nothing will save a man but a legal administrator.
Joseph Smith, HC 5:259

Priesthood is as eternal as God himself.
Joseph Smith, HC 5:555

How vain and trifling have been our spirits, our conferences, our councils, our meetings, our private as well as public conversations—too low, too mean, too vulgar, too condescending for the dignified characters of the called and chosen of God.
Joseph Smith, HC 3:295-96

The rain descends upon the evil and upon the good; but the rights of the priesthood are conferred, and the doctrine of the priesthood distills as the dews of heaven upon the souls of those only that receive it in God's own appointed way.
Joseph F. Smith, JD 24:176

No men or body of men can gather together or work independently and originate the holy priesthood upon the earth. To do so would be a greater miracle than for one to originate life in dead matter.
James E. Talmage, CR 4/20:102

The powers and functions of the Holy Priesthood, as manifested in mortality today, are but as the foothills compared with the towering peaks beyond.
James E. Talmage, CR 4/18:161

No greater responsibility can be given to a young man

than to hold the priesthood of God.
N. Eldon Tanner, CR 10/70:93

No man, young or old, who holds the priesthood of
God can honor that priesthood without honoring and
respecting womanhood.
N. Eldon Tanner, CR 4/73:124

The future of the world depends on how we magnify
the office which we hold in the priesthood.
N. Eldon Tanner, CR 10/75:112

The Priesthood is not instituted for the purpose of
personal aggrandizement or personal honor, but it is
for the accomplishment of certain purposes of which
the Lord is the Author and Designer, and in which the
dead, the living, and the unborn are interested.
John Taylor, JD 19:121

Priesthood and people are inseparable.
Orson F. Whitney, CR 4/07:110

The priesthood of any people is really a definition of
the God in which that people believes.
John A. Widtsoe, CR 10/21:48

See also: Leadership, Responsibility

PRINCIPLES

A frequent recurrence to fundamental principles is
essential to the security of individual rights and the
perpetuity of free government.
Anon. Charles H. Hart, CR 4/13:75

Principles never change, through all the eternities, but
policies do, and should, according to circumstances.
Charles W. Penrose, CR 10/13:24

That which is wrong under one circumstance, may be,
and often is right under another.
Joseph Smith, HC 5:135

It is a dangerous thing for our young people to

conceive the idea that they must sacrifice principle at the shrine of policy.
Moses Thatcher, JD 24:299

God's work is progressive. It changes its appearance, but never its principles.
Orson F. Whitney, CR 10/16:56

When people stand for principle, and know by their faith in God that the principle is true, it is always a mark of true greatness.
Levi Edgar Young, CR 4/19:29

PRIORITIES

Some men take the cream of their energy for making money, and when they come to the Lord's work, they've got nothing but skim milk.
Marvin O. Ashton, CR 4/46:91

Too often we are involved in the thick of thin things.
Anon. A. Theodore Tuttle, CR 10/71:95

See that the things that matter most . . . are not at the mercy of things that matter least.
Anon. A. Theodore Tuttle, CR 10/71:95

PRISON

Rigor and seclusion will never do as much to reform the propensities of men as reason and friendship. Murder only can claim confinement or death.
Joseph Smith, HC 6:205

PROBLEMS

A wholesome sense of humor will be a safety valve that will enable you to apply the lighter touch to heavy problems and to learn some lessons in problem solving that "sweat and tears" often fail to dissolve.
Hugh B. Brown, CR 4/68:100

Within the gospel of Jesus Christ may be found the solution to every problem confronting us.
Harold B. Lee, CR 4/66:64

I think we have set the pace for the solution of all the problems that concern the human race.
Levi Edgar Young, CR 4/13:72

See also: Adversity, Mortality, Trials

PROCRASTINATION

Procrastination—thou wretched thief of time and opportunity!
Spencer W. Kimball, CR 4/66:75

One of the most cruel games anyone can play with self is the "not yet" game—hoping to sin just a bit more before ceasing; to enjoy the praise of the world a little longer before turning away from the applause; to win just once more in the wearying sweepstakes of materialism; to be chaste, but not yet; to be good neighbors, but not now.
Neal A. Maxwell, CR 10/74:16

Joshua didn't say choose you next year whom you will serve; he spoke of "this day," while there is still daylight and before the darkness becomes more and more normal.
Neal A. Maxwell, CR 10/74:15

The people of the antediluvian world waited one day too long.
Orson Pratt, JD 18:228

To procrastinate is the greatest gamble on earth. You gamble with death.
Eldred G. Smith, CR 10/53:32

As the time of repentance is procrastinated, the ability to repent grows weaker. Neglect of opportunity in holy things brings a forfeit of the chance.
Eldred G. Smith, CR 10/49:12

Procrastination . . . is the thief of eternal life.
  Joseph Fielding Smith, CR 4/69:121

Upon the great face of the world's time piece is only written one word, and that is *now.*
  Reed Smoot, CR 10/04:48

There is nothing that steals man's time, his talents, his vigor, his energy, even his prospects of salvation, in greater degree than the crime of procrastination. Procrastination means making an appointment with opportunity and then asking her to come around some future time.
  Reed Smoot, CR 10/07:58

PROFANITY

Profanity is the effort of a feeble brain to express itself forcibly.
  Spencer W. Kimball, CR 10/74:7

No parent can consistently teach faith in Christ who profanes the name of Deity.
  David O. McKay, CR 10/48:119

PROGRESS

Let us strive for progress down the road of goodness and freedom.
  Ezra Taft Benson, CR 4/73:51

Free agency is the impelling force of the soul's progress.
  David O. McKay, CR 4/50:32

There can be no progress without liberty.
  Henry D. Moyle, CR 4/59:97

One of our most unfortunate weaknesses is that we sometimes think we are under sentence to remain forever as we presently are.
  Sterling W. Sill, CR 10/63:80

When you climb up a ladder, you must begin at the bottom and ascend step by step, until you arrive at the top; and so it is with the principles of the gospel.
Joseph Smith, HC 6:306-7

All the minds and spirits that God ever sent into the world are susceptible of enlargement.
Joseph Smith, HC 6:311

See also: Eternal Progression, Improvement, Success

PROPHECY

Prophecy is but history in reverse—a divine disclosure of future events.
Ezra Taft Benson, CR 10/73:89

The gift of prophecy will not save any man. It is not a saving principle; it is a gift.
John W. Taylor, CR 4/00:26

See also: Prophets, Revelation

PROPHETS

If there was but one prophet on the face of the earth, and he had no followers, but stood alone in the midst of the nations of the earth, his warnings would be followed by terrible results if they were disregarded by those who heard them. The Lord does not look upon men according to their numbers.
George Q. Cannon, JD 20:246

Few people will ever have the privilege of locking arms and striding with a prophet, but everyone may have the privilege of following him.
William J. Critchlow, Jr., CR 4/63:30

Let us not wait for another prophet to come and tell us what we already know.
Richard L. Evans, CR 10/52:127

The words of a prophet, when spoken by the Spirit of God, are the words of God.
   J. Golden Kimball, CR 4/28:79

Astronomers have sought knowledge through study, but prophets through faith.
   Spencer W. Kimball, CR 4/62:59

No father, no son, no mother, no daughter should get so busy that he or she does not have time to study the scriptures and the words of modern prophets.
   Spencer W. Kimball, CR 4/76:71

Even in the Church many are prone to garnish the sepulchres of yesterday's prophets and mentally stone the living ones.
   Spencer W. Kimball, ACR 8/73:76

Those who try to guess ahead of time as to who is going to be the next president of the Church are just gambling as they might be on a horse race, because only the Lord has the time table.
   Harold B. Lee, CR 10/72:129

If you want to know what the Lord would have the Saints know and to have his guidance and direction for the next six months, get a copy of the proceedings of this conference, and you will have the latest word of the Lord as far as the Saints are concerned.
   Harold B. Lee, CR 10/73:168

When God makes the prophet he does not unmake the man.
   Anon. David O. McKay, CR 4/07:11

Always when the Lord has had a people on the earth whom he has recognized as his own, he has led them by living prophets to whom he has given guidance from heaven.
   Mark E. Petersen, CR 10/72:150

The predicament in which we find ourselves today has not come about for want of an adequate guide, but

rather for want of a listening ear.
Marion G. Romney, CR 10/71:68

God works not only by direct methods; He works also
by indirect methods; not only through the schools of
the prophets, but once in a while He raises up a
prophet that was not reared in the school of the
prophets.
B. H. Roberts, CR 4/08:110

It is an easy thing to believe in the dead prophets, but
it is a greater thing to believe in the living prophets.
Marion G. Romney, CR 4/53:125

A prophet who walks alone can do little more than
mark time.
Robert L. Simpson, CR 10/75:18

A prophet [is] a prophet only when . . . acting as such.
Joseph Smith, HC 5:265

If any person should ask me if I were a prophet, I
should not deny it, as that would give me the lie; for,
according to John, the testimony of Jesus is the spirit
of prophecy.
Joseph Smith, HC 5:215

The Lord will never forsake his servants who stand at
the head of his Church.
Alma Sonne, CR 4/66:77

A prophet not only prophesies of things that will
happen. A prophet, by the exercise of faith, causes
things to happen.
A. Theodore Tuttle, CR 10/75:33

Our salvation is contingent upon our belief in a living
prophet and adherence to his word.
A. Theodore Tuttle, CR 4/73:12

God will select a prophet, a mouthpiece, a bearer of
His priesthood, a teacher of His truth, without asking
any man's permission; but He will never foist upon

any man, nor upon any set of men or women, a leader, a presiding officer that they are not willing to sustain.
Orson F. Whitney, CR 4/09:74

The Lord never did bring judgment upon any people of any generation until he raised up prophets to warn them of the impending danger.
Wilford Woodruff, JD 23:82

There never was a Prophet on the earth but what was subject to passions, as we are.
Brigham Young, JD 8:352

See also: Leadership

PUNISHMENT

I believe that there are no real punishments except those which we bring upon ourselves.
J. Reuben Clark, Jr., CR 4/54:9

There can be no forgiveness without real and total repentance and there can be no repentance without punishment. This is as eternal as is the soul.
Spencer W. Kimball, CR 4/75:116

Often, very often, we are punished as much by our sins as for them.
Boyd K. Packer, ACR 8/74:84

See also: Judgment, Plan of Salvation

PURITY

Purity is power.
Hugh B. Brown, CR 4/64:56

No one will ever be comfortable without being clean.
Richard L. Evans, CR 10/70:88

The foundation of growth in this Church is purity, with faith in God.
David O. McKay, CR 10/18:48

The brightest light and the clearest signal come from the cleanest instrument.
H. Burke Peterson, CR 10/74:99

Be [as] pure in your sphere as God is pure in His.
Daniel H. Wells, JD 23:310

See also: Forgiveness, Repentance

REACTIVATION

I am convinced that there are many in the Church who are committing spiritual suicide, . . . and if we can only recognize the cry of distress in time, we will be the means of saving souls.
Harold B. Lee, CR 4/72:117

It is better for us to save our own boys who are being misled at home, than it is for us to go out into the world and spend years of time and endless means in order to gather in a few people from the world.
Joseph F. Smith, CR 10/02:87

We spend hundreds of thousands of dollars and give the time and the lives of our Elders to spread the Gospel abroad, and why should we not be just as anxious to save those at home who have drifted away or have become cold in the Gospel?
Abraham O. Woodruff, CR 4/02:33

REASON

Reason is all right when intelligently used.
Joseph Fielding Smith, CR 4/16:71

Reason is only compatible with truth. Error and evil, no matter how one may try to reason with it, still remain error and evil leading to chaos.
John H. Vandenberg, CR 4/73:43

When reason is joined with truth, there is convincing logic that sets up the path in our hearts that leads

upward and onward to a nobler life.
John H. Vandenberg, CR 4/73:43

REBIRTH

If we are to come into the Church and Kingdom of God it must be by some such means as birth. We must be born into the Kingdom of God. We cannot walk into it; we cannot run or jump into it, or drop into it, or grow up into it; we must be born into it. We must go through the door, and the door is baptism.
Rudger Clawson, CR 10/30:77

We can be born again as many times as we please. And each time we can be born better.
Sterling W. Sill, CR 4/75:63

That man that has none of the blood of Abraham (naturally) must have a new creation by the Holy Ghost.
Joseph Smith, HC 3:380

See also: Baptism, Conversion

RECORDS

No report form, no filled-out slip, no written word can ever take the place of a kind and patient teacher.
Theodore M. Burton, CR 4/67:44

The objective is not counting the sheep but feeding them.
Marion D. Hanks, CR 10/70:57

The only true record that will ever be made of my service in my new calling will be the record that I may have written in the hearts and lives of those with whom I have served and labored, within and without the Church.
Harold B. Lee, CR 10/72:19

When we come to stand before the bar of God, to be

judged out of the things which are written in the books, we may find a difference between those things which are written in the books here and the things which are written in the books there.

Joseph F. Smith, CR 4/99:68

RELIGION

Theology may be only diction, but religion requires action.

Hugh B. Brown, CR 10/62:41

Religion has to do not only with the internal life of man, but with his eternal life, which will be a continuation of identity and personality into the spiritual realm of immortality.

Hugh B. Brown, CR 10/62:42

Religion is the means by which a man may achieve tranquillity of spirit without internal anguish or external disaster.

Hugh B. Brown, CR 10/62:42

I have not thought that religion was like a Sunday garment, to be worn on Sunday in the meeting house, tabernacle, chapel or church, and to be laid aside again on Monday morning. I have never had that idea of religion, I do not have it now.

George Q. Cannon, JD 17:122

True religion is the activated love of God and of neighbor.

ElRay L. Christiansen, CR 10/61:10

To talk about a religion to a Latter-day Saint that has no living Prophet or apostle in it—that has no living God in it, who can and will speak to his creature, man, in this day, is to talk to him of an egg without meat, a body without spirit, an eye without sight, or an ear without hearing.

Orson Hyde, JD 5:143

A man who considers his religion a slavery has not begun to comprehend the real nature of religion.
  J. Golden Kimball, CR 4/11:70

The great need of the American home today is more religion.
  David O. McKay, CR 4/65:7

The real test of any religion is the kind of man it makes.
  David O. McKay, CR 10/63:8

True religion cannot be worn only on Sundays.
  David O. McKay, CR 4/58:130

True religion has three manifestations; first, the thought, the feeling, the mental and spiritual attitude of the individual toward his God; second, worship; and third, service to one's fellows.
  David O. McKay, CR 4/29:98

All true morality is supported by and finds its basis in religion.
  Stephen L Richards, CR 10/23:47

Our religion is not a thing apart from our life. It is incorporated in it, and forms a part of the very tissue and sinews of our being.
  Stephen L Richards, CR 4/17:137

One of the most important parts of real religion is to qualify ourselves to govern our own lives effectively and righteously.
  Sterling W. Sill, CR 10/63:78

The religion of Christ itself is not so much a set of ideas as it is a set of activities.
  Sterling W. Sill, CR 4/71:35

A religious system is of but little account when it possesses no virtue nor power to better the condition of people, spiritually, intellectually, morally and physically.
  Lorenzo Snow, JD 26:371

The religion of God is not a religion of ignorance.
John Taylor, JD 25:214

True religion refreshes the heart as gentle rains the
parched and thirsting soil.
Moses Thatcher, JD 26:307

As the value of a coin is largely determined by its
purchasing power, so the value of a religion may be
partly determined by its cost and largely by the
blessings it will bring.
Moses Thatcher, JD 26:308

I suspect that one real difference between religion and
ethics is in the manner in which truth is used.
John A. Widtsoe, CR 10/21:47

The world needs the flaming fire of religion to replace
the dead husks of ethics.
John A. Widtsoe, CR 4/34:116

No religion is of much value unless it has a practical
application.
Clifford E. Young, CR 10/49:65

REPENTANCE

No matter what your past has been, you have a
spotless future.
Hugh B. Brown, CR 10/69:103

To the repentant sinner the Church, and we
individuals, have all forgiveness; to the repentant
sinner we open our arms in welcome; but against the
sin which he commits the Church must always war.
J. Reuben Clark, Jr., CR 4/34:95

Whatever the penalties, however long or arduous the
process, even humbling in sackcloth and ashes,
repentance is the only course.
James A. Cullimore, CR 10/71:91

There is nothing wrong with an individual that faith

and repentance will not cure.
  Alvin R. Dyer, CR 10/69:56

If it were not for repentance and forgiveness, I would
become discouraged and discontinue my labors.
  J. Golden Kimball, CR 10/10:32

The supplication of Enos is written with a pen of
anguish and on the paper of faith and with a
willingness to totally prostrate himself that he might
receive forgiveness.
  Spencer W. Kimball, ACR 8/74:45

Repentance is a principle and not merely an
expression of penitent grief.
  John Longden, CR 4/65:128

The first step to repentance is to quit sinning.
  Francis M. Lyman, CR 4/99:38

The difference between the Gospel law and the
manner of our observance of it, represents the things
which we have to repent of.
  George F. Richards, CR 4/13:82

When men sin, there is no substitute for repentance.
  Stephen L Richards, CR 10/58:8

A universal, genuine, and permanent repentance
would close up our jails, do away with our reform
schools, prevent our nervous breakdowns, fill our
churches, redeem our souls, and restore harmony,
peace, and happiness to the world.
  Sterling W. Sill, CR 10/64:111-12

Repentance is God's cure for every disease that
plagues our lives.
  Sterling W. Sill, CR 10/64:112

So long as we put off either the forsaking or confessing
of our sins, just so long do we delay the day of our
redemption.
  Marion G. Romney, CR 10/55:125

There is no other remedy for the ills of this world but repentance.
George Albert Smith, CR 10/22:97

Daily transgression and daily repentance is not that which is pleasing in the sight of God.
Joseph Smith, HC 3:379

Nothing is so much calculated to lead people to forsake sin as to take them by the hand, and watch over them with tenderness.
Joseph Smith, HC 5:23-24

Repentance is the very essence of change; it embodies the powerful principle of obedience to God's law and discipline of self. When applied to our lives it provides a cleansing joy which surges through us.
John H. Vandenberg, CR 10/72:25

Without repentance we cannot grow spiritually.
Rulon S. Wells, CR 4/07:44

Every doctrine of the Church, every sermon that has been preached from this pulpit, has to do with faith in God and repentance from sin.
Rulon S. Wells, CR 10/33:48

You cannot constantly be sinning a little and repenting, and retain the Spirit of the Lord as your constant companion.
Brigham Young, JD 9:220

See also: Forgiveness

REPUTATION

I like to think of reputation as a window, clearly exhibiting the integrity of one's soul.
O. Leslie Stone, CR 10/75:60

RESPONSIBILITY

Great blessings are always accompanied by great

responsibility.
Victor L. Brown, ACR 8/71:68

There probably is too much talk about rights and not
enough talk about responsibility.
Thorpe B. Isaacson, CR 4/60:60

Young men do not usually become inactive in the
Church because they are given too many significant
things to do.
Spencer W. Kimball, CR 4/76:68

Man's responsibility is correspondingly operative with
his free agency.
David O. McKay, CR 10/65:8

See also: Leadership, Priesthood

RESURRECTION

The change of nature from the chill of winter to the
beauty of spring, as nature comes to life each year,
recalls the change from the gloom and despair of
Gethsemane to the glorious event of the resurrection.
Howard W. Hunter, CR 4/75:56

Like the stillness of death Old Winter has held all
vegetable life in his grasp, but as Spring approaches
the tender life-giving power of heat and light compels
him to relinquish his grip, and what seems to have
been dead comes forth in newness of life, refreshed,
invigorated, strengthened after a peaceful sleep.
David O. McKay, CR 4/39:115

The disappointment of hopes and expectations at the
resurrection would be indescribably dreadful.
Joseph Smith, HC 6:51

It is no more incredible that God should *save* the dead,
than that he should *raise* the dead.
Joseph Smith, HC 4:425

All your losses will be made up to you in the

resurrection, provided you continue faithful. By the vision of the Almighty I have seen it.
Joseph Smith, HC 5:362

If anyone supposes that any part of our bodies, that is, the fundamental parts thereof, ever goes into another body, he is mistaken.
Joseph Smith, HC 5:339

RETROGRESSION

If his faith is not kept radiant by good works, he will be tempted to lower his ideals to the level of his conduct. This is retrogression.
Hugh B. Brown, CR 4/63:7

It is written in the eternity of our God that every soul must progress that does not retrograde.
George Q. Cannon, JD 26:87

There is no such thing as standing still.
Heber J. Grant, CR 4/02:80

If we are not drawing towards God in principle, we are going from him and drawing towards the devil.
Joseph Smith, HC 4:588

There is no man or woman who can stand still any great length of time. In this path over which we are moving we are very likely to go backward if we undertake to stand still or act indifferently.
Lorenzo Snow, CR 4/98:12

REVELATION

Had any man accepted the ancient scripture in the days of Noah but refused to follow the revelation that Noah received and failed to board the ark, he would have been drowned.
Ezra Taft Benson, CR 10/72:54

So long as men believe there can be no revelation,

they will make no attempt to tune in.
  Hugh B. Brown, CR 10/61:94

It appears to me that men are trying to speak *for* God
instead of letting God speak for *himself.*
  Theodore M. Burton, CR 10/71:73

When God speaks to man, his words can become
either a curse or a blessing.
  Theodore M. Burton, CR 10/72:48

The stars, those rounded orbits of light, the sun and
the moon and the heavens declare the glory of God,
but they do not declare his will.
  Charles A. Callis, CR 4/39:126

From the day that God established this Church to the
present the stream of revelation has continued to flow
uninterruptedly. It flows pure for us to drink at until
we are filled to repletion; and if we do not drink, it is
our own fault.
  George Q. Cannon, JD 10:344

No circumstances will arise in this country that will
affect the welfare of this people, whether from a
religious, a political, a financial, a social, business,
scientific, or any other standpoint, but what Almighty
God is bound to have something to say in regard to
them.
  Matthias F. Cowley, CR 10/00:19

We need revelation for the calling of officers in the
Church. Men should not be called merely through
impression.
  J. Golden Kimball, CR 4/10:55

As we incline our hearts to our Heavenly Father and
his Son Jesus Christ, we hear a symphony of sweet
music sung by heavenly voices proclaiming the gospel
of peace.
  Spencer W. Kimball, CR 4/74:65

Mother's intuition . . . is a form of divine guidance in

202

its purest and simplest form.
Harold B. Lee, CR 10/66:118

The trouble with us today, there are too many of us
who put question marks instead of periods after what
the Lord says.
Harold B. Lee, CR 10/72:130

God reveals himself or he remains forever unknown.
Bruce R. McConkie, CR 10/69:80

I know there is revelation in the Church because I
have received revelation.
Bruce R. McConkie, CR 10/72:21

We cannot be turned from the wheat of the word of
God, to the chaff that comes from the wisdom of man.
Joseph W. McMurrin, CR 4/06:27

If we live worthy of divine guidance, as we are
privileged to do, we shall not go very far astray.
Joseph F. Merrill, CR 10/40:77

All the doctrines we have in our Church are scriptural,
but they have not been taken from the scriptures, they
have come direct from the Almighty by revelation in
our time.
Charles W. Penrose, JD 22:162

I wonder sometimes if we are willing to pay the price
for an answer from the Lord.
H. Burke Peterson, CR 10/73:13

Reading about new revelation, prophecies and
ministrations of angels is one thing, but actually
receiving them is entirely another thing.
Orson Pratt, JD 12:251

The voice of Him that spake to the waves of
Gennesaret, and commanded them to be still, speaks
to us, and while dark clouds and the thunderings and
lightnings roll over the political horizon, yet in the
hearts, in the homes, and in the habitations of the just
there is peace.
Franklin D. Richards (1821, 1849-1899), JD 24:282

When the word of the Lord comes to us, it tells us
what to do, when to do, and how to do.
Franklin D. Richards (1821, 1849-1889), CR 10/98:32

Prayer is the means by which men communicate with
God. Revelation is the means by which God
communicates with men.
Marion G. Romney, CR 4/64:122

We never can comprehend the things of God and of
heaven, but by revelation.
Joseph Smith, HC 5:344

We have no new commandment to give, but
admonish Elders and members to live by every word
that proceedeth forth from the mouth of God.
Joseph Smith, HC 5:404

Much instruction has been given to man since the
beginning which we do not possess now.
Joseph Smith, HC 2:18

God hath not revealed anything to Joseph, but what
He will make known unto the Twelve, and even the
least Saint may know all things as fast as he is able to
bear them.
Joseph Smith, HC 3:380

The things of God are of deep import; and time, and
experience, and careful and ponderous and solemn
thoughts can only find them out.
Joseph Smith, HC 3:295

The reason we do not have the secrets of the Lord
revealed unto us, is because we do not keep them.
Joseph Smith, HC 4:479

No man can receive the Holy Ghost without receiving
revelations.
Joseph Smith, HC 6:58

All things whatsoever God in his infinite wisdom has
seen fit and proper to reveal to us, while we are

dwelling in mortality, in regard to our mortal bodies, are revealed to us in the abstract, and independent of affinity of this mortal tabernacle, but are revealed to our spirits precisely as though we had no bodies at all; and those revelations which will save our spirits will save our bodies.

Joseph Smith, HC 6:313

We never inquire at the hand of God for special revelation only in case of there being no previous revelation to suit the case.

Joseph Smith, HC 1:339

The Lord deals with this people as a tender parent with a child, communicating light and intelligence and the knowledge of his ways as they can bear it.

Joseph Smith, HC 5:402

It is my meditation all the day, and more than my meat and drink, to know how I shall make the Saints of God comprehend the visions that roll like an overflowing surge before my mind.

Joseph Smith, HC 5:362

I could explain a hundred fold more than I ever have of the glories of the kingdoms manifested to me in the vision, were I permitted, and were the people prepared to receive them.

Joseph Smith, HC 5:402

The man who possesses the spirit of revelation can realize whether he is a sinner, whether he is prone to evil, whether he is magnifying his standing before the Lord, or not, better than a man that has not the Spirit of the Lord in him.

Joseph F. Smith, CR 4/12:7

Any doctrine, whether it comes in the name of religion, science, philosophy, or whatever it may be, if it is in conflict with the revealed word of the Lord, will fail.

Joseph Fielding Smith, CR 10/52:60

If we are not receiving revelations from God today it is not His fault.
Reed Smoot, CR 4/15:93

We stand upon the rock of revelation, and though the rains may beat and the winds may blow, we shall not be moved unless we get frightened and abandon the refuge of safety, and be swept into the whirlpool of man-made doctrine.
James E. Talmage, CR 10/18:60

We ought to be a better people than those who make no pretentions to be guided by divine revelation.
John Taylor, JD 25:87

Revelation does not depend upon books. It is an eternal principle, a perennial, ever-flowing fountain. Books may come and books may go, but revelation goes on forever.
Orson F. Whitney, CR 10/25:102

[God] is not going to bestow the great mysteries of the invisible worlds upon us. We know too much already unless we do better.
Brigham Young, JD 13:264

The supreme test of religion is revelation. No religion can be persuasive unless it relies on the principle of revelation.
Levi Edgar Young, CR 4/59:31

Every grove can be a sacred grove, every mountaintop a Sinai.
S. Dilworth Young, CR 4/75:147

Causing the bosom to burn is another way of saying that feeling is a big part of the process of revelation.
S. Dilworth Young, CR 4/76:34

See also: Holy Ghost, Inspiration, Prophecy

REVERENCE

Reverence is the fundamental virtue in religion.
David O. McKay, CR 10/56:6

Reverence is profound respect mingled with love.
David O. McKay, CR 10/56:6

If reverence is the highest, then irreverence is the lowest state in which a man can live in the world.
David O. McKay, CR 10/56:6

The greatest manifestation of spirituality is reverence; indeed, reverence is spirituality.
David O. McKay, CR 10/56:6

An irreverent man is not a believing man.
David O. McKay, CR 10/51:180

If there were more reverence in human hearts, there would be less room for sin and sorrow.
David O. McKay, CR 10/55:5

The principle of self-control lies at the basis of reverence.
David O. McKay, CR 10/50:163

REVOLUTION

God is about to perform through His Saints, one of the mightiest revolutions that has ever been effected in the earth. He is able to establish his kingdom—a new order of things, an entirely different rule and power among men.
George Q. Cannon, JD 22:281

The kingdom of God must be a continuing revolution against the norms of the society that fall below the standards that are set for us in the gospel of Jesus Christ.
Harold B. Lee, CR 10/70:110

I intend to lay a foundation that will revolutionize the whole world.
Joseph Smith, HC 6:365

See also: War

REWARDS

Must people be rewarded for doing right?
Spencer W. Kimball, CR 4/74:128

The mere fact that we receive the ordinances in no sense guarantees that we will receive these rewards.
Bruce R. McConkie, CR 10/55:13

The approval of a man's own conscience is his richest earthly reward.
John Henry Smith, CR 10/10:9

See also: Judgment

RIGHTEOUSNESS

Righteousness and hate cannot dwell in the same heart, no matter how great the righteousness nor how little the hate.
J. Reuben Clark, Jr., CR 10/38:136

Only righteousness pays dividends.
Spencer W. Kimball, CR 4/74:129

There can be no true happiness and no true joy, in my judgment, without righteousness.
Stephen L Richards, CR 4/20:98

We can legislate until doomsday but that will not make men righteous.
George Albert Smith, CR 10/49:6

There is a close connection between the righteousness or sinfulness of mankind and the occurrence of natural phenomena.
James E. Talmage, CR 10/23:49

See also: Obedience

SABBATH

If we don't keep the sabbath day holy, he may still be our God, but we may not be his people.
Milton R. Hunter, CR 4/47:60

The Savior knew that the ox gets in the mire on the Sabbath, but he knew also that no ox deliberately goes into the mire every week.
Spencer W. Kimball, CR 10/53:55

People look at you six days in the week to see what you mean on the Sabbath.
David O. McKay, CR 10/22:79

Observance of the Sabbath is an indication of the depth of our conversion.
Mark E. Petersen, CR 4/75:72

Sabbath observance will help us to more fully remain unspotted from the world.
Mark E. Petersen, CR 4/75:70

No person can disregard the Lord's day without suffering serious spiritual consequences.
John Wells, CR 4/32:111

SACRAMENT

To partake of the sacrament unworthily is to take a step toward spiritual death.
David O. McKay, CR 10/29:14-15

See also: Jesus Christ

SACRIFICE

Only if you sacrifice for a cause will you love it.
Victor L. Brown, CR 10/75:100

There is no blessing without sacrifice, but it isn't a sacrifice unless it hurts.
Theodore M. Burton, CR 10/62:66

If we understood completely the designs of the Lord, we would be more patient in our suffering and would not complain as much as we so often do when hardships come and we are asked to sacrifice.
Theodore M. Burton, CR 4/71:109

No great principle has ever been established among the children of men without costly sacrifices.
George Q. Cannon, JD 25:268

Whenever the Lord has a great blessing for one of his children, he puts that son or daughter in the way to make a great sacrifice.
Harold B. Lee, CR 4/47:50

The real secret of the success of the Lord's program here on earth, or anywhere else for that matter, is sacrifice.
Hartman Rector, Jr., CR 4/75:82-83

We talk a great deal about sacrifices, when strictly there is no such thing; it is a misnomer—it is a wrong view of the subject, for what we do in the kingdom of God is the best investment we can possibly make. It pays the best, which ever way we may look at it, it is the principle of all others to be coveted—to be appreciated—and is the best investment we can make of all that pertains to us in this life.
Daniel H. Wells, JD 4:253

Sacrifice creates love.
John H. Vandenberg, CR 4/71:73

Sacrifice is the evidence of true love.
John A. Widtsoe, CR 4/43:38

SAFETY

Some mistakenly think the pathway of safety is somewhere between the path of righteousness and the road to destruction.
Marvin J. Ashton, CR 4/71:12

The future safety of the world depends not so much
upon the changing of defenses as upon the changing
of men's way of thinking and acting.
  David O. McKay, CR 10/45:131

SAINT

A saint is not necessarily a person who is perfect, he is
a person who strives for perfection—one who tries to
overcome those faults and failings which take him
away from God. A true saint will seek to change his
manner of living to conform more closely to the ways
of the Lord.
  Theodore M. Burton, CR 10/73:151

To be a Saint is an individual work, and it is out of
the power of God, angels, or men to make a Saint of a
man who is determined to be a sinner.
  Heber C. Kimball, JD 22:250

You cannot be a Saint without the fellowship of the
Spirit of God.
  George Teasdale, CR 10/03:51

A Saint is a man who is sanctified.
  George Teasdale, CR 10/98:39

If the Lord has any friends on the earth they are the
Saints of God, and if the Saints of God have any
friends anywhere, they consist of the God of Israel and
the heavenly hosts, and the spirits of just men made
perfect.
  Wilford Woodruff, CR 4/80:7

If a man will do a wrong thing wilfully, he is not a
Saint.
  Brigham Young, JD 13:177

There are and always have been a great many in this
Church that are not Saints. There are more
"Mormons" than Saints; and there are different

degrees and grades of "Mormons" and of Saints.
There are many that are "Mormons" that are not
Saints.
Brigham Young, JD 6:194

See also: Latter-day Saints

SALVATION

There is only one way to salvation, that is by active
participation.
Hugh B. Brown, CR 4/63:89

Salvation is essentially a family affair, and full
participation in the plan of salvation can be had only
in family units.
Hugh B. Brown, CR 10/66:103

Salvation of the whole eternal family of God is the
goal toward which we have been working and
preparing ourselves from the very beginning.
Theodore M. Burton, CR 4/75:105

The greatest work we can do is to so live that we
ourselves shall be saved, that our own acts shall be
correct, and our will and desires and passions be
brought into subjection to the will of God.
George Q. Cannon, JD 20:291

A man who cannot save himself through the power of
God; a man who cannot save his wife and children,
cannot bring to Christ the souls of men in the world.
Rudger Clawson, CR 4/01:8

No man could have permanent joy without salvation.
Rudger Clawson 4/31:19

Salvation is personal and individual.
Bruce R. McConkie, CR 10/69:80

Salvation is a family affair.
Bruce R. McConkie, CR 4/59:118

Salvation does not come by reading about religion, by learning that holy men in former days had spiritual experiences. It is not found through research in musty archives; it does not spring forth as the result of intellectual dialogues about religious matters. Salvation is born of obedience to the laws and ordinances of the gospel.
Bruce R. McConkie, CR 10/68:135

To work out one's salvation is not to sit idly by dreaming and yearning for God miraculously to thrust bounteous blessings into our laps.
David O. McKay, CR 4/57:7

The saved individual is the supreme end of the Divine Will.
David O. McKay, CR 10/69:8

There is no salvation without work.
David O. McKay, CR 10/09:90

Salvation is a process of gradual development.
David O. McKay, CR 4/57:7

Salvation is an individual affair.
David O. McKay, CR 4/57:4

God is a great economist. Everything that can be saved will be saved, and only that which cannot be saved will be lost.
Charles W. Penrose, CR 10/16:19

If persons separate themselves from the Lord's church, they thereby separate themselves from his means of salvation, for salvation is through the Church.
Mark E. Petersen, 4/73:159

Salvation is not a free gift. The offer is free indeed, through the atonement of the Savior. But its enjoyment must be earned.
Mark E. Petersen, CR 10/73:141

It is possible to lose our salvation by default.
Mark E. Petersen, CR 10/73:142

Men are not saved by virtue of their testimony alone.
Hartman Rector, Jr., CR 4/74:158

If we were to do as well as we know, our salvation would be secure.
George F. Richards, CR 4/36:77

Holding a particular office in the Church will never save a person.
Marion G. Romney, CR 4/73:116-17

No man on the earth will ever be saved by the Gospel unless he believes it.
Hyrum M. Smith, CR 4/04:51

We have not hung our hope of salvation upon a single peg, nor do we rely for our salvation upon one word of scripture.
Hyrum M. Smith, CR 10/10:66

Salvation means a man's being placed beyond the power of all his enemies.
Joseph Smith, HC 5:392

When we have power to put all enemies under our feet in this world, and a knowledge to triumph over all evil spirits in the world to come, then we are saved.
Joseph Smith, HC 5:387

Salvation cannot come without revelation.
Joseph Smith, HC 3:389

Where there is no kingdom of God there is no salvation.
Joseph Smith, HC 5:257

Temporal salvation is just as important in its sphere as spiritual salvation is in its sphere. In fact, temporal salvation and spiritual salvation are so closely united that they cannot be separated. There is no dividing line.
Joseph Fielding Smith, CR 4/33:22

One good act will never save a person, but one bad act

may be the means of his downfall and damnation.
Reed Smoot, CR 10/03:64

Our salvation is contingent upon our belief in a living prophet and adherence to his word.
A. Theodore Tuttle, CR 4/73:12

It is service that saves.
A. Theodore Tuttle, CR 4/72:150

There can be no salvation in compulsion.
Rulon S. Wells, CR 4/30:69

Salvation is rather synonymous to the term education.
Rulon S. Wells, CR 10/31:62

See also: Eternal Life, Eternity, Exaltation

SATAN

Satan is not dead yet.
Ezra T. Benson, JD 6:263

✗Never has the devil been so well organized.
Ezra Taft Benson, CR 10/70:21

Satan shall be bound, and will have no more power over the hearts of the children of men. . . . But do you know that we can bind the Lord also by our wickedness?
Melvin J. Ballard, CR 4/24:149

Those who teach that there is no devil or who declare him to be a figment of the imagination used only to frighten people are either ignorant of the facts or they themselves are deceived.
ElRay L. Christiansen, CR 10/74:29

✗ When the Holy Ghost is really within us, Satan must remain without.
ElRay L. Christiansen, CR 10/74:30

Satan will be bound by the power of God; but he will be bound also by the determination of the people of

God not to listen to him, not to be governed by him. The Lord will not bind him and take his power from the earth while there are men and women willing to be governed by him.

George Q. Cannon, CR 10/97:65

We don't have to dive to the depths of filth and perversion to know the destructive powers of Satan.

Vaughn J. Featherstone, ACR 8/74:133

To deny the existence of Satan and the reality of his evil power and influence is as foolish as ignoring the existence of electricity.

David B. Haight, CR 4/73:84

Whoever said that sin was not fun? Whoever claimed that Lucifer was not handsome, persuasive, easy, friendly?

Spencer W. Kimball, CR 4/67:66

It is not necessary . . . that Satan extinguish our light, if he can simply keep it dim.

Neal A. Maxwell, ACR 8/74:13

The adversary has no stronger weapon against any group of men or women in this Church than the weapon of thrusting in a wedge of disunity, doubt, and enmity.

David O. McKay, CR 10/67:6

Resist the devil, and he will flee from you.

David O. McKay, CR 10/58:88

We are all a part of a great battle that is covering the face of the earth—a conflict between the brethren of the priesthood and the legions of Satan.

H. Burke Peterson, CR 10/74:97

The devil can adapt himself to the belief of any person.

Orson Pratt, JD 13:73

Satan is the master of deceit.

Robert L. Simpson, CR 10/72:145

Satan has spread the false rumor that confidences are rarely kept.
Robert L. Simpson, CR 4/72:33

✗ Satan cannot stand cheerfulness which comes from righteous living.
Eldred G. Smith, CR 10/52:62

As well might the devil seek to dethrone Jehovah, as overthrow an innocent soul that resists everything which is evil.
Joseph Smith, HC 4:605

There are so many fools in the world for the devil to operate upon it gives him the advantage oftentimes.
Joseph Smith, HC 6:184

If it was possible for Satan to destroy this work, he would have accomplished it in its infancy.
Reed Smoot, CR 4/02:24

If Satan and his hosts were bound today and no longer able to work personally upon the earth, evil would go on for a long time, because he has very able representatives in the flesh.
James E. Talmage, CR 10/14:104

Of all the imitators, of all the counterfeiters, Satan is the chief, for he has had the greatest experience and the longest training and he is a skillful salesman; he not only knows how to manufacture his spurious goods, but how to put them upon the market.
James E. Talmage, CR 10/12:127

The devil did not make this earth. It never belonged to him, and never will.
Wilford Woodruff, JD 11:243

See also: Evil, Sin, Transgression

SCIENCE

The notion that science is all fact and religion all faith

is fiction.
  Hugh B. Brown, CR 10/69:105

If science is built upon facts, its architect is faith.
  Hugh B. Brown, CR 10/62:42

Just as a scientific experiment must be performed
under proper conditions of heat and light and pressure
and absolute cleanliness, so the spiritual experiment
must be performed with a pure heart, with a desire to
know the truth, with a clean body and a clean mind,
in order that the one experimenting may not shut
himself off from the very things he desires to know.
  J. Reuben Clark, Jr., CR 4/34:95

I wonder how much our presumed scientific
knowledge, so-called, has cost us in faith.
  J. Reuben Clark, Jr., CR 4/57:86

Science has done marvelous things for man, but it
cannot accomplish the things he must do for himself,
the greatest of which is to find the reality of God.
  Howard W. Hunter, CR 10/74:139

The apparent conflict . . . between religion and
science, arises from two definite causes: an imperfect
knowledge of science on the one hand and an
imperfect knowledge of religion on the other.
  Rulon S. Wells, CR 4/29:104

There is no true religion without true science, and
consequently there is no true science without true
religion.
  Brigham Young, JD 17:52

  See also: Evolution

SCRIPTURE

I have noticed myself among the Latter-day Saints
that where the people of God pay attention to the
written word, they are always better prepared to hear

the oral instructions of the servants of God.
George Q. Cannon, CR 10/97:38

There is a definite relationship between our solving problems and living happy, joyful lives and our understanding and knowledge of scriptures.
Paul H. Dunn, ACR 8/71:64

There is nothing that qualifies a man so much for preaching the gospel of the Lord Jesus Christ as to study the revelations that the Lord has seen fit to give us in our day.
Heber J. Grant, 10/25:6

No father, no son, no mother, no daughter should get so busy that he or she does not have time to study the scriptures and the words of modern prophets.
Spencer W. Kimball, CR 4/76:71

In the final analysis, the gospel of God is written, not in the dead letters of the scriptural records, but in the lives of the Saints.
Bruce R. McConkie, CR 10/68:135

If all men reading the scriptures were moved upon by the power of the Holy Ghost, we wouldn't have hundreds of churches claiming that they have the truth.
LeGrand Richards, CR 10/66:43

These ancient scriptures are impressive and edifying, but it is the modern scripture by which we are bound and will be judged.
Marion G. Romney, CR 10/72:115

We must not allow the holy scriptures to sit on our shelves unopened while we continue to starve to death spiritually.
Sterling W. Sill, CR 4/72:159

One of the shortcomings of even the holy scriptures is that they are not automatic. That is, they will not work unless we do.
Sterling W. Sill, CR 10/73:79

Should the scriptures fall open at almost any place, they would very likely reveal the remedy for all problems, even present-day conditions.
Eldred G. Smith, CR 10/68:40

Though we understand Homer and Shakespeare and Milton, . . . if we have failed to read the scriptures we have missed the better part of this world's literature.
George Albert Smith, CR 10/17:43

There is more to be learned in five minutes reading in the holy scriptures, more that is worthy of retention in the memory, more that will be helpful if we remember and obey them, than we can find in reading all of the six best sellers in every month in the year.
Hyrum M. Smith, CR 10/17:38

Search the scriptures, search the prophets, and learn what portion of them belongs to you.
Joseph Smith, HC 1:282

We are differently situated from any other people that ever existed upon this earth; consequently those former revelations cannot be suited to our conditions.
Joseph Smith, HC 2:52

I have a key by which I understand the scriptures. I enquire, what was the question which drew out the answer, or caused Jesus to utter the parable?
Joseph Smith, HC 5:261

Peter penned the most sublime language of any of the apostles.
Joseph Smith, HC 5:392

𝓐 I know of no time in the history of this Church, of no time in the history of the world, when it has been more important or necessary for the people to know the will of God, and to make themselves acquainted with that which he has revealed.
Joseph Fielding Smith, CR 10/34:63

We believe that the scriptures are very simple to understand, if we can only get the theologians to leave

them alone and not confuse us with explanations.
James E. Talmage, CR 4/17:66

It is hard to understand why so many people are
prepared to accept facts as recorded by historians in
secular history and yet refuse to accept ecclesiastical
history as recorded in the scriptures.
N. Eldon Tanner, CR 10/72:133-34

What would be the use of the scriptures to us if there
were no living men having authority to officiate in the
ordinances of the house of God.
George Teasdale, CR 10/97:11

All scriptures set the moral code for mankind to live
by.
John M. Vandenberg, CR 10/74:135

There are some of our Elders who will argue
themselves into false doctrine by giving an undue
preference to one scripture and passing over others
equally as important.
Brigham Young, JD 11:283

If the word of God does not mean what it says, no
man or woman can explain it without a direct
revelation from Heaven.
Brigham Young, JD 12:299

There are the Old and New Testaments, the Book of
Mormon, and the Book of Doctrine and Covenants,
which Joseph has given us, and they are of great
worth to a person wandering in darkness. They are
like a lighthouse in the ocean, or a finger-post which
points out the road we should travel.
Brigham Young, JD 8:129

See also: Bible, Book of Mormon, Revelation

SECRETS

The reason we do not have the secrets of the Lord

revealed unto us, is because we do not keep them.
Joseph Smith, HC 4:479

When I find a person that is good at keeping a secret,
so am I; you can keep yours, and I mine.
Brigham Young, JD 4:288

See also: Gossip

SECURITY

For the righteous the gospel provides a warning before
a calamity, a program for the crises, a refuge for every
disaster.
Ezra Taft Benson, CR 10/73:90

There is no security in unrighteousness.
Ezra Taft Benson, CR 10/50:147

People who are willing . . . to trade freedom for
security, are sowing the seeds of destruction and
deserve neither freedom nor security.
Ezra Taft Benson, CR 10/54:120

No enduring society was ever founded on the basis of
physical comfort.
Albert E. Bowen, CR 10/37:85

Preparation, character, competence are still the source
of security.
Richard L. Evans, CR 4/68:87

Security is not born of inexhaustible wealth but of
unquenchable faith.
Spencer W. Kimball, CR 4/73:153

Church membership is not passive security but
continuing opportunity.
Neal A. Maxwell, CR 4/74:163

The real source of security of our nation rests in the
well-ordered and properly conducted home.
David O. McKay, CR 4/35:113

The only security that there is for perfect life, for advancement, for progress, for peace, lies in the gospel of Jesus Christ.
Stephen L Richards, CR 10/20:70

SELF-CONTROL

The soul that is worth the honor of earth, is the soul that resists desire.
Anon. David O. McKay, CR 4/57:9

A man may perform a mission; he may do innumerable good works; his name may be heralded throughout the Church and to the nations of the earth, and the people may accept it as that of a great and mighty man; but if that man does not conquer himself and live in strict accordance with the principles of the Gospel, his position will only increase his condemnation.
George Q. Cannon, JD 20:291

To conquer and subdue the earth is futile if we fail to conquer and subdue ourselves.
ElRay L. Christiansen, CR 10/64:130

The only conquest that brings satisfaction is the conquest of self.
Gordon B. Hinckley, CR 10/70:65

If you fail to gain absolute self-control, you have failed in the greatest victory of life.
Antoine R. Ivins, CR 4/52:73

If you do not overcome your passions here, you have got to do it there.
Heber C. Kimball, JD 3:22

Soul development results from complete control of physical desires and passions.
David O. McKay, CR 10/56:7

As in eternal life, so in self-mastery, there is no one

great thing which a man may do to obtain it; but
there are many little things by observing which
self-control may be achieved.
  David O. McKay, CR 4/32:64

Those who desire to win self-mastery must do it by
constant application.
  David O. McKay, CR 4/15:105

There is nothing that gives a man such strength of
character as the sense of self-conquest, the realization
that he can make his appetites and passions serve him.
  David O. McKay, CR 4/68:8

A man who cannot control his temper is not very
likely to control his passions, and no matter what his
pretensions in religion, he moves in daily life very
close to the animal plane.
  David O. McKay, CR 10/63:89

If we are to control our children, we must first learn to
control ourselves.
  H. Burke Peterson, ACR 8/73:63

The most inspiring thing about the life of Jesus was
not his ability to quiet the storm or control the
tempest, but his absolute control of himself.
  Sterling W. Sill, CR 10/63:78

One of the most important parts of real religion is to
qualify ourselves to govern our own lives effectively
and righteously.
  Sterling W. Sill, CR 10/63:78

No man is safe unless he is master of himself; and
there is no tyrant so merciless or more to be dreaded
than an uncontrollable appetite or passion.
  Joseph F. Smith, JD 25:55

A person cannot be free who does not restrain himself.
  Rulon S. Wells, CR 10/12:23

The greatest mystery a man ever learned, is to know
how to control the human mind, and bring every

faculty and power of the same in subjection to Jesus Christ; this is the greatest mystery we have to learn while in these tabernacles of clay.
Brigham Young, JD 1:46-47

If you first gain power to check your words, you will then begin to have power to check your judgment, and at length actually gain power to check your thoughts and reflections.
Brigham Young, JD 6:98

I do not know of a more absolute monarch that ever reigned on earth than the one who has perfect control over his passions.
Brigham Young, JD 13:244

The real test of the strength of civilization is in the moral capacity of the rank and file of the citizens to give up the pleasures of the present for greater rewards in the future.
Levi Edgar Young, CR 10/36:67-68

See also: Character, Self-Discipline

SELF-DISCIPLINE

Individual spiritual development cannot be realized without self-discipline.
ElRay L. Christiansen, CR 4/71:26

God has written the score which we are to perform. Our prophet is our director. With effort and with harmony we can stir the world and "crown him lord of all," if we have the will to discipline ourselves with that restraint which comes of true testimony.
Gordon B. Hinckley, CR 10/61:116

If you want to be successful or outstanding in any field of endeavor, it is important that you determine while young to be a great boy, and not wait to be a man to be a great man; and then have the courage and

strength and determination to discipline yourself,
apply self-control and self-mastery.
    N. Eldon Tanner, CR 4/75:112

   See also: Passions, Self-control

SELF-RELIANCE

Usually the Lord gives us the overall objectives to be
accomplished and some guidelines to follow, but he
expects us to work out most of the details and
methods.
    Ezra Taft Benson, CR 4/65:121

The Lord will not do for us what we can and should
do for ourselves.
    Ezra Taft Benson, CR 10/45:164

The responsibility for feeding our souls is one of the
primary do-it-yourself projects that God himself has
put into our hands.
    Sterling W. Sill, CR 4/72:158

I never ask the Lord to do a thing I could do myself.
    John Taylor, JD 1:27

A reasonable amount of self-reliance is a good thing, is
a pillar of strength in any human character. But when
a man relies wholly upon himself and seeks no help
from the divine helper, he is leaning upon a broken
reed, however mighty he may think himself.
    Orson F. Whitney, CR 10/27:147

The only heaven for you is that which you make
yourselves.
    Brigham Young, JD 4:57

If we ever walk in streets paved with gold, . . . we will
have placed it there ourselves.
    Brigham Young, JD 8:354-55

The Lord will help those who help themselves to do
right.
    Brigham Young, JD 1:92

SELFISHNESS

A hermit is one who suffers from the extreme of selfishness.
Robert D. Hales, CR 10/75:139

Man never stands alone unless his own desires are selfishness, independence, and egotism.
Spencer W. Kimball, ACR 8/73:77

The man who is ambitious for personal gain and personal advantage is never a happy man, for before him always are the receding horizons of life that will ever mock his attempts at acquisition and conquest. That man who serves unselfishly is the man who is the happy man.
Harold B. Lee, CR 4/47:49-50

Selfishness is the root from which spring most human ills and suffering.
David O. McKay, CR 10/45:132

Selfishness is at the bottom of all law violation, of depravity, and crime.
Joseph F. Merrill, CR 4/32:116

Let us pull the weeds from our own gardens and remove every root of selfishness, every seed of bitterness and everything that is not good, and live together, as brethren and sisters as the Lord has commanded, in love and humility and in obedience to his laws and commandments.
Charles W. Penrose, CR 4/02:54

Selfishness is at the root of nearly all the disorders that afflict us.
Mark E. Petersen, CR 10/71:64

Avarice and selfishness mastermind all sin and crime.
John H. Vandenberg, CR 10/65:131

Some men think they are economical when, as a matter of fact, they are only stingy.
Rulon S. Wells, CR 4/38:70

When you loose yourself in service there is more of you to find the!

SERVICE

The gospel plan is a plan of continuous service.
Joseph Anderson, ACR 8/73:33

No one ever lifted someone else without stepping toward higher ground.
Marvin J. Ashton, CR 10/73:131

Don't simply give—give of yourself. Don't take without taking part.
Marvin J. Ashton, CR 4/74:50

We were not chosen nor set apart to rule, but chosen and set apart to serve.
Theodore M. Burton, CR 4/61:126

Consecrated service is the road to the hearts of men.
Charles A. Callis, CR 10/36:106

The best of life is expressed in service to others.
Charles A. Callis, CR 4/42:43

The only road to heaven is the road of service.
Charles A. Callis, CR 4/39:126

When we are resurrected, I doubt that we will be asked, "How many positions did you hold?" but rather, "How many people did you help?"
ElRay L. Christiansen, CR 4/67:45

In the service of the Lord, it is not where you serve but how.
J. Reuben Clark, Jr., CR 4/51:154

When working for self we acquire the things that will perish, but that which we do through faith in God, with an eye single to his glory, with love and brotherly kindness for each other, that will be placed to our credit, and no one can take it from us.
Anthon H. Lund, CR 4/08:13

When you labor for your brother you always get the chief reward yourself.
Francis M. Lyman, CR 4/15:47

God is not viewed from the standpoint of what we
may get from him, but what we may give to him.
  David O. McKay, CR 10/53:10

The most worthy calling in life is that in which man
can serve best his fellow man.
  David O. McKay, CR 4/61:131

ᐣ Man's greatest happiness comes from losing himself
for the good of others.
  David O. McKay, CR 10/63:8

There is more spirituality expressed in giving than in
receiving.
  David O. McKay, CR 10/36:104

The greatest spiritual blessing comes from helping
another.
  David O. McKay, CR 10/36:104

If you would be happy, render a kind service, make
somebody else happy.
  David O. McKay, CR 10/36:104-5

We will become mightier and more powerful in our
own right in direct proportion to the service and
contribution we make to strengthen the Church.
  Henry D. Moyle, CR 4/62:90

People do not really care how much you know until
they know how much you care.
  Hartman Rector, Jr., CR 10/73:136

This gospel we have received is one of sacrifice, service
and self-abnegation from beginning to end. That is
what constitutes the straight and narrow way that
leads to life eternal.
  George F. Richards, CR 10/20:39

The true test of devotion is giving of one's self.
  Stephen L Richards, CR 4/49:141

It is not what we receive that enriches our lives, it is
what we give.
  George Albert Smith, CR 4/35:46

Our eternal happiness will be in proportion to the way that we devote ourselves to helping others.
George Albert Smith, CR 10/36:71

Every kind act that we perform for one of our Father's children is but a permanent investment made by us that will bear eternal dividends.
George Albert Smith, CR 4/14:13

All I can offer the world is a good heart and a good hand.
Joseph Smith, HC 5:498

When you find yourselves a little gloomy, look around you and find somebody that is in a worse plight than yourself.
Lorenzo Snow, CR 4/99:2

There is no real happiness in having or getting, but only in giving.
N. Eldon Tanner, CR 4/67:104

If we take good care of one another, God will take care of us.
John Taylor, CR 4/80:65

It is service that saves.
A. Theodore Tuttle, CR 4/72:150

The happiest people on earth are those who contribute to the welfare of their neighbors and friends.
John Wells, CR 10/34:31

All who labor for Zion, her interests and welfare, both at home and abroad, are the best paid people in all the world. Their names are upon the payroll, and the Lord is the paymaster.
Rulon S. Wells, CR 4/15:135

It is better to feed nine unworthy persons than to let one worthy person—the tenth, go hungry. Follow this

rule and you will be apt to be found on the right side
of doing good.
Brigham Young, JD 16:44

See also: Love

SEX

The Lord did not give sex to man for a plaything.
Spencer W. Kimball, CR 4/74:7

Seeking the pleasure of conjugality without
willingness to assume the responsibilities of rearing a
family is one of the onslaughts that now batter at the
structure of the American home.
David O. McKay, CR 4/69:5

See also: Adultery, Immorality

SEX EDUCATION

Have you ever asked yourselves why this sudden urge
to teach sex in a public way? Is someone afraid that
the rising generation will not know how to reproduce
itself, and that the race thereby may die out?
Mark E. Petersen, CR 4/69:63

SIGNS OF THE TIMES

Obedience to the commandments here referred to—
the principles and ordinances of the gospel—
constitute the sure and only means of escaping the
impending calamity.
Marion G. Romney, CR 10/58:97

The Lord hath set the bow in the cloud for a sign that
while it shall be seen, seedtime and harvest, Summer
and Winter shall not fail; but when it shall disappear,
woe to that generaion, for behold the end cometh
quickly.
Joseph Smith, HC 5:402

See also: Latter Days, Millennium

SILENCE

Silence is a thousand times better than words, especially if those words are not in wisdom.
Brigham Young, JD 13:244

SIMPLICITY

I never design to communicate any ideas but what are simple.
Joseph Smith, HC 5:529

The truth is frequently shocking just because of its simplicity and consequent grandeur.
James E. Talmage, CR 4/15:121

The test of truth is simplicity.
John A. Widtsoe, CR 4/21:37

SIN

You cannot do wrong and feel right.
Ezra Taft Benson, CR 10/71:26

We live in a day of slick, quiet, and clever sins.
Ezra Taft Benson, CR 4/63:110

Sin creates disharmony with God and is depressing to the spirit.
Ezra Taft Benson, CR 10/74:91

A little sin will not stay little.
ElRay L. Christiansen, CR 10/74:29

When you find a man that has fallen by the wayside, you can trace in his course the neglect of some duty or the violation of some covenant which he has made with his God.
Matthias F. Cowley, CR 10/98:9

Whatever is detrimental to health and happiness, or whatever impairs effectiveness or efficiency, is clearly

wrong, morally wrong, spiritually wrong, as well as physically wrong.
Richard L. Evans, CR 4/57:13

There are thousands of things that could destroy you mentally, morally, physically, spiritually, and not one of them is worth it.
Richard L. Evans, CR 4/70:16

I am grateful for the Church because it calls sin by its real name.
Vaughn J. Featherstone, ACR 8/74:73

Sin is the barbed wire that cuts and scars, and sometimes leaves the poison of its rust within the wound, to destroy the body and to contaminate the soul.
Charles H. Hart, CR 10/13:43

Sin brings its proper punishment, sooner or later and in total, so that one is stupid indeed to choose to do the wrong things.
Spencer W. Kimball, CR 4/74:126

Perhaps never before has the world accepted sin so completely as a way of life.
Spencer W. Kimball, CR 4/72:29

Sin comes when communication lines are down—it always does, sooner or later.
Spencer W. Kimball, CR 4/72:29

The heaviest burden that one has to bear in this life is the burden of sin.
Harold B. Lee, CR 4/73:177

Trees that can stand in the midst of the hurricane often yield to the destroying pests that you can scarcely see with a microscope.
David O. McKay, CR 10/11:57

We may be charitable and forbearing to the sinner, but must condemn the sin.
David O. McKay, CR 10/39:102

Sin can stun the conscience as a blow on the head can
stun the physical senses.
    David O. McKay, CR 10/29:15

Often, very often, we are punished as much by our
sins as for them.
    Boyd K. Packer, ACR 8/74:84

Personal sin is as much an apostasy from Christ as an
acceptance of false doctrines and man-made rituals.
    Mark E. Petersen, CR 4/65:35

Sin is disease and the testimony of Christ procures
immunity from that disease.
    Stephen L Richards, CR 10/25:118

When men sin, there is no substitute for repentance.
    Stephen L Richards, CR 10/58:8

Most of the suffering distress endured by people of this
earth is the result of unrepented and unremitted sin.
    Marion G. Romney, CR 4/59:11

No sin is born fully grown.
    Sterling W. Sill, CR 4/65:88

In fighting against God we are sinning against
ourselves.
    Sterling W. Sill, CR 10/64:111

We should never think of sin as a plaything, but as our
most deadly enemy.
    Sterling W. Sill, CR 10/64:113

We are training ourselves to love sin. We pay money
to see it being committed on the screen; we read about
it in books, magazines, and newspapers; and quite
naturally we absorb it into our lives.
    Sterling W. Sill, CR 10/64:111

Little evils do the most injury to the Church.
    Joseph Smith, HC 5:140

One good act will never save a person, but one bad act

may be the means of his downfall and damnation.
Reed Smoot, CR 10/03:64

We sometimes boast of being in the land of the free, the home of the brave. Nevertheless, we are not free until we have overcome evil—until we liberate ourselves from the bondage of sin.
Rulon S. Wells, CR 4/30:70

There are different sins, and there are different degrees of sin of the same kind.
Orson F. Whitney, CR 4/11:44

See also: Evil, Repentance, Satan, Transgression

SINCERITY

It is not enough for us to be sincere in what we support. We must be right!
Marion G. Romney, CR 10/60:75

SLANDER

The Church must be judged by what it is, not by what people say of it.
Anthony W. Ivins, CR 10/23:143

The source of slander may be found in a depraved nature. It is a weed the roots of which find richest sustenance in a soul that is seeking to destroy his fellows.
David O. McKay, CR 10/31:11

SLAVERY

The loss of freedom with the consent of the enslaved, or even at their request, is nonetheless slavery.
Marion G. Romney, CR 4/66:98

There are some people who think they are always in slavery and bondage unless they are trying to get

themselves into trouble; and they think there is no true liberty only in acting like the devil.
Erastus Snow, JD 22:150

I do not know a worse degree of slavery than to be afraid to think for yourself and speak what you believe.
George Teasdale, CR 4/01:34

See also: Freedom, Sin

SMILE

You can recognize the Spirit of Christ within you when you speak to one another or speak of another person with a warm smile instead of with a frown or scowl.
Theodore M. Burton, CR 10/74:77

SMITH, JOSEPH (See JOSEPH SMITH)

SOCIETY

Without just laws by which society may be controlled and the rights of the people protected, and honest, conscientious men to administer them, the Church cannot exist.
Anthony W. Ivins, CR 4/19:81

There is an inseparable connection between the keeping of the commandments and the well-being of society.
Neal A. Maxwell, CR 10/74:15

The great purpose of the Church is to translate truth into a better social order.
David O. McKay, CR 10/66:85

See also: Civilization, World

SORROW

People often get themselves into trouble—not by trying to make themselves miserable, but by looking for the right things in the wrong way.
Richard L. Evans, ACR 8/71:72

When we do not keep active in the Church, we can be frozen by the chill winds of disappointment and sorrow.
Neal A. Maxwell, ACR 8/74:13

When the darkness comes, let us remember that the night brings out the stars as sorrows show us the truth; and the insight that comes through pain and disappointment may be the insight into the value of what we are.
Levi Edgar Young, CR 10/32:58-59

SPEAKING

Someone said that a person's brain was a most marvelous mechanism, that it begins to work at one's birth and never stops until one stands up and attempts to speak in public.
Anon. Clifford E. Young, CR 10/49:65

For a speech to be immortal it does not need to be everlasting.
Hugh B. Brown, CR 4/56:103

There is nothing more delightful to the human mind, properly constituted, than to listen to the words of life and salvation spoken under the inspiration of the Holy Ghost; they are sweeter than the sweetest honey, and more satisfying than the best and most nutritious food.
George Q. Cannon, JD 11:98

The greatest and the most wonderful preacher among the Latter-day Saints is the man or the woman who lives the gospel of the Lord Jesus Christ.
Heber J. Grant, CR 10/22:185

We seldom get into trouble when we speak softly.
    Gordon B. Hinckley, CR 4/71:82

The greatest joy, the greatest peace, and greatest
happiness I have ever had in my life have come when
speaking under the spirit of testimony.
    J. Golden Kimball, CR 4/35:35

It takes lots of courage to say always what you think.
The trouble is, we think things sometimes we ought
not to say.
    J. Golden Kimball, CR 4/10:53

Great sermons have been preached in this Church by
the simple shaking of hands.
    J. Golden Kimball, CR 4/99:53

I never like to preach to Latter-day Saints who have
already been over-fed with such spiritual nourishment
and are not hungry; it seems like wasting effort.
    J. Golden Kimball, CR 4/09:36

I have the idea, but it is not yet clothed.
    J. Golden Kimball, CR 4/98:42

My brethren and sisters, I have been hanging on the
hook so long during this conference that I am nearly
exhausted. I have had some wonderful thoughts, but
you waited so long they have nearly all oozed out of
me.
    J. Golden Kimball, CR 4/21:178

When President Brigham Young came, with the
pioneers, he was sick, and prostrated in the wagon in
which he was riding, he rose and saw this valley, and
said: "This is the place: Drive on." He did not preach
for an hour over it.
    J. Golden Kimball, CR 4/15:78-79

My sermons will be no better than the lives of the
members of my family.
    Harold B. Lee, CR 10/72:176

I am not concerned about how much you remember

in words of what has been said here. I am concerned about how it has made you feel.
Harold B. Lee, CR 10/72:176

We never make any headway by mere exhortation.
Harold B. Lee, CR 4/72:117

A better service can sometimes be given to others by speaking well of them, or, if you cannot speak well of them, by refraining from speaking of them at all, than by any physical aid which we can give.
David O. McKay, CR 10/19:79

Less talking behind the pulpit will have a salutary effect upon those who face it.
David O. McKay, CR 10/55:5

Oratory is addressed to the ears; eloquence given of God, to the heart.
James E. Talmage, CR 4/14:93

A man can never speak upon anything that is wrong, so long as he confines himself to the limits of truth.
John Taylor, JD 7:194

Nothing to my mind can be greater sacrilege in the sight of the Almighty than to undertake to speak in His name without the inspiration of His spirit.
Moses Thatcher, JD 26:303-4

Every doctrine of the Church, every sermon that has been preached from this pulpit, has to do with faith in God and repentance from sin.
Rulon S. Wells, CR 10/33:48

I do not care a fig for eloquence if it be obscure. . . . A man is never eloquent when he tries to be. Eloquence comes from being earnest, from having in our hearts a desire to bless the people and feed them with the bread of life.
Orson F. Whitney, CR 4/10:59

You cannot hide the heart, when the mouth is open.
Brigham Young, JD 6:74

If you are tried and tempted and buffeted by Satan, keep your thoughts to yourselves—keep your mouths closed; for speaking produces fruit, either of good or evil character.
Brigham Young, JD 7:268

See also: Example, Preaching, Teaching

SPIRIT

What the spirit is to the body, God is to the spirit.
David O. McKay, CR 4/67:134

There is no such thing as immaterial matter. All spirit is matter, but is more fine or pure, and can only be discerned by purer eyes. We cannot see it, but when our bodies are purified, we shall see that it is all matter.
Joseph Smith, HC 5:393

God never had the power to create the spirit of man at all. God himself could not create himself.
Joseph Smith, HC 6:311

Spirit is a substance; it is material, but it is more pure, elastic and refined matter than the body; it existed before the body, can exist in the body; and will exist separate from the body, when the body will be mouldering in the dust; and will in the resurrection be again united with it.
Joseph Smith, HC 4:575

The mind is an attribute of the spirit.
James E. Talmage, CR 10/22:69

SPIRITS

There never was a time when there was not spirits; for they are co-equal with our Father in heaven.
Joseph Smith, HC 6:311

SPIRITUAL

The only thing which places man above the beasts of the field is his possession of spiritual gifts.
David O. McKay, CR 10/51:9

All that is good is spiritual.
Henry D. Moyle, CR 10/60:20

Our spiritual senses are more delicately balanced than any of our physical senses.
Boyd K. Packer, CR 4/63:108

It is the business of man to find the spiritual meaning of earthly things.
John A. Widtsoe, CR 4/22:96

See also: Spirituality

SPIRITUAL DEATH

Carelessness around electric power lines can be suddenly lethal. Carelessness around priesthood power lines can be slowly lethal, producing a lingering, withering, spiritual death.
William J. Critchlow, Jr., CR 4/64:31

To partake of the sacrament unworthily is to take a step toward spiritual death.
David O. McKay, CR 10/29:14-15

Through the blood of the Lamb we have amnesty from spiritual death if we keep the commandments of the Lord.
Boyd K. Packer, CR 4/63:109

See also: Hell

SPIRITUALITY

As the relish with which one enjoys a meal depends upon the appetite he brings to the table more than upon the quality and variety of food placed before him, so the degree of enjoyment and assimilation of

spiritual refreshment will depend upon whether or not we "hunger and thirst" as enjoined by the Savior.
Hugh B. Brown, CR 4/63:6

The key to true spirituality is priesthood genealogy.
Theodore M. Burton, CR 10/66:35

The Spirit of God will not dwell in a man that has evil desires and does not try to quench them.
George Q. Cannon, CR 10/97:68

Individual spiritual development cannot be realized without self-discipline.
ElRay L. Christiansen, CR 4/71:26

✻ Spirituality is as essential to a man's soul as vitamins are to his body.
Thorpe B. Isaacson, CR 10/65:95

✻ Activity is the soul of spirituality.
Harold B. Lee, CR 10/71:129

The Latter-day Saints are as sensitive to the movements and operations of the Spirit of the Lord as the thermometer is to the presence of the heat and cold.
Francis M. Lyman, CR 4/01:48-49

I know people who have written books about religion but who have about as much spirituality as a cedar post.
Bruce R. McConkie, CR 4/71:100

The greatest manifestation of spirituality is reverence; indeed, reverence is spirituality.
David O. McKay, CR 10/56:6

Spirituality [is] the highest acquisition of the soul.
David O. McKay, CR 4/61:7

There is more spirituality expressed in giving than in receiving.
David O. McKay, CR 10/36:104

Spirituality is the consciousness of victory over self
and of communion with the Infinite.
David O. McKay, CR 4/58:6

Every noble impulse, every unselfish expression of
love, every brave suffering for the right; every
surrender of self to something higher than self; every
loyalty to an ideal; every unselfish devotion to
principle; every helpfulness to humanity; every act of
self-control; every fine courage of the soul, undefeated
by pretence or policy, but by being, doing, and living
of good for the very good's sake—that is spirituality.
David O. McKay, CR 4/58:6

A physician judges the health by the appetite, and our
spirituality may be judged the same way.
Sterling W. Sill, CR 4/57:109

The deepest expression of spirituality is love.
Robert L. Simpson, CR 10/64:94

A man never finds perfect peace, never reaches afar
unless he penetrates to some degree the unseen world,
and reaches out to touch the hands, as it were, of those
who live in that unseen world, the world out of which
we came, the world into which we shall go.
John A. Widtsoe, CR 10/38:129

> *See also:* Holy Ghost, Spiritual

STEWARDSHIP

No man has a right to administer in anything to
which he has not been appointed.
Charles W. Penrose, CR 10/10:64

I will inform you that it is contrary to the economy of
God for any member of the Church, or any one, to
receive instruction for those in authority, higher than
themselves.
Joseph Smith, HC 1:338

God will hold you responsible for those whom you might have saved had you done your duty.
John Taylor, JD 20:23

There never was a man in the Church of God that received the spirit of any calling whereunto he was called until he started to administer in that calling.
John W. Taylor, CR 10/00:31

The teacher, or deacon that fulfills his duties is a great deal more honorable than a president or any of the twelve that does not.
John Taylor, JD 21:209

Heaven will not perform the labour that it has designed us to perform.
Brigham Young, JD 9:244

See also: Leadership, Priesthood

SUCCESS

The secret of succeeding comes from doing the right thing at the right time and in the right way, and God will show you the way.
Melvin J. Ballard, CR 4/33:127

Nothing can keep us from success when we are doing the Lord's work.
Theodore M. Burton, CR 10/71:76

A wise man looks at the results—not the tool.
Theodore M. Burton, CR 4/61:127

Every one, no matter who he may be, who works on the theory that there are some things in life that are not worth his best effort, and who accordingly slights his work, will never be truly successful.
J. Reuben Clark, Jr., CR 4/36:62

The great success which attended the ministry of Jesus Christ was due to His strict obedience to the will of the Father.
Rudger Clawson, CR 10/02:51

The greater the value of the object desired, the greater the effort required in its attainment.
Rudger Clawson, CR 10/14:78

The word *can't* is false doctrine in the Mormon Church.
Paul H. Dunn, CR 4/72:107

There aren't any careless, easy shortcuts that go anywhere that anyone who knew what he was doing would really want to go.
Richard L. Evans, CR 10/70:88

The trouble with a great many people is, they are not willing to *pay the price;* they are not willing to make the fight for success in the battle of life.
Heber J. Grant, CR 10/19:5

A man who so lived that those who knew him best, loved him most, and whom God loved, was entitled to be crowned with the wreath of success although he might die in poverty.
Heber J. Grant, CR 4/32:12

A successful mother is one who is never too tired for her sons and daughters to come and share their joys and their sorrows with her.
Harold B. Lee, CR 8/72:91

The steps of a ladder may be trivial in themselves, but we have to use them if we want to get to the top.
Anthon H. Lund, CR 10/15:9

No other success can compensate for failure in the home.
David O. McKay, CR 4/64:5

No one is really successful who is not happy.
Hartman Rector, Jr., CR 4/73:86

We should seek the success of the inner man, now that our affluent society has furbished the outer man so extensively.
Franklin D. Richards (1900, 1960-   ), CR 10/70:79

I have found it wise to survey large fields but cultivate small ones.
Franklin D. Richards (1900, 1960-   ), CR 10/64:77

Let us realize that the privilege to work is a gift, that the power to work is a blessing, that the love of work is success.
Franklin D. Richards (1900, 1960-   ), CR 10/69:124

No permanent success comes to those who do not possess good character.
Stephen L Richards, CR 10/52:101

There is nothing like trying except success, and trying earnestly means success.
Joseph F. Smith, CR 10/98:26

If you wish to achieve financial success, if you wish to be happy, if you wish to be healthy, if you would be morally clean, if you wish to find religious peace of mind, there is only one sure way, and that is the straight and narrow path—the way of honor, the way of industry, of moderation, simplicity, and virtue.
N. Eldon Tanner, CR 4/75:112

If you want to be successful or outstanding in any field of endeavor, it is important that you determine while young to be a great boy, and not wait to be a man to be a great man; and then have the courage and strength and determination to discipline yourself, apply self-control and self-mastery.
N. Eldon Tanner, CR 4/75:112

If a man achieves worldly success and does not blend into his life a program of self-improvement to bring about a sensible balance, he no doubt will end up as a failure.
John H. Vandenberg, CR 10/72:26

The success of this life is not measured at the end of it by what we have, but rather by what we are.
Rulon S. Wells, CR 10/12:25

No man can rise very high who lives by earthly things alone.
John A. Widtsoe, CR 4/40:38

Greatness of life is won only when men regulate and order the affairs and acts of their lives by an understanding of the great spiritual purpose of man's existence.
John A. Widtsoe, CR 4/22:97

Those who think that they can succeed without praying, try it, and I will promise them eternal destruction, if they persist in that course.
Brigham Young, JD 7:205

I claim there never has been anything accomplished by a man unless he dreamed dreams and had visions of greater things.
Levi Edgar Young, CR 4/13:73

See also: Failure, Greatness, Improvement, Progress

TEACHERS

The teacher and the truth taught should be of the same pattern.
Hugh B. Brown, CR 4/63:89

The greater the teacher, the greater the pupil may become.
Theodore M. Burton, CR 4/61:128

No report form, no filled-out slip, no written word can ever take the place of a kind and patient teacher.
Theodore M. Burton, CR 4/67:44

Great teachers are always underpaid.
Thorpe B. Isaacson, CR 10/63:96

No greater responsibility can rest upon any man, than to be a teacher of God's children.
David O. McKay, CR 10/16:57

See also: Education, Teaching

TEACHING

No man can teach the Word of Wisdom by the Spirit of God who does not live it.
Heber J. Grant, CR 10/37:130

No man can teach the gospel of Jesus Christ under the inspiration of the living God and with power from on high unless he is living it.
Heber J. Grant, CR 4/38:15

Teaching by precept, without example, is mighty poor teaching.
Heber J. Grant, CR 4/11:24

There is no teaching of morality without personality.
David O. McKay, CR 10/69:86

The home is the teaching unit of the Church.
A. Theodore Tuttle, CR 10/69:131

As well might a man try to teach chemistry or algebra without knowing them as to undertake the teaching of the things of God without the Spirit of God.
Rulon S. Wells, CR 10/31:63

Teaching is unfolding the divine spark within every person into its fullest majestic purpose and scope.
Levi Edgar Young, CR 4/51:29

TEMPLE

➤ If members holding the priesthood reject the opportunity to go to the temple regularly, they reject the very God who made them and with whom they have covenanted to always remember him and to walk in his ways.
Theodore M. Burton, CR 4/71:110

⚐ The temple of God is the connecting link that connects the heavens with the earth.
Rudger Clawson, CR 4/33:77-78

248

We work for those who live and also for the dead, thus following in the footsteps of our Lord and Master.
Francis M. Lyman, CR 4/11:15

Parents who themselves have lightly regarded their temple covenants can expect little better from their children.
Harold B. Lee, CR 4/57:22

I wish to call your attention to your temple work. . . . Do not put it off until you are entirely ready, because if you do, perhaps you will not get ready at all.
Marriner W. Merrill, CR 10/99:64-65

When a seal is put upon the father and mother, it secures their posterity, so that they cannot be lost, but will be saved by virtue of the covenant of their father and mother.
Joseph Smith, HC 5:530

Do not watch for iniquity in each other, if you do you will not get an endowment, for God will not bestow it on such.
Joseph Smith, HC 2:309

There is nothing that will ever come into your family life that is as important as the sealing blessings of the temple and then keeping the covenants made in connection with this order of celestial marriage.
Joseph Fielding Smith, CR 4/72:13

None of us need think that we shall be benefitted by covering up our uncleanness and expect that we shall be sanctified by the outer ordinances of the temple of our God, when the inner man is corrupt.
Erastus Snow, CR 4/80:90

See also: Genealogy, Marriage

TEMPLE MARRIAGE (See MARRIAGE)

TEMPORAL

There is a spiritual side to the gospel, and there is a
temporal side, and it is difficult to find a dividing line.
Rudger Clawson, CR 4/06:29

I contend that every man that holds the priesthood
ought to be a saviour temporally as well as spiritually,
for we are in duty bound to try to save our natural
lives.
Heber C. Kimball, JD 8:109

I would not give a cent for a religion that was not a
part of, and did not affect, the temporal life of every
adherent.
Reed Smoot, CR 4/07:30

Prayers are all well enough; but a little flour, a little
pork, a little beef, sugar, store goods, and temporal
comforts are a great deal better than all our prayers
without this material assistance.
John Taylor, CR 4/80:68

TEMPTATION

We should never go into a place, save we are sent on a
spiritual mission, where there would be any likelihood
that the Spirit of the Lord could not go with us.
J. Reuben Clark, Jr., CR 4/53:55

Do not tempt temptation.
Richard L. Evans, CR 4/58:76

No one ever fell over a precipice who never went near
one.
Richard L. Evans, CR 4/70:16

There are no sins charged to our account because we
are tempted, provided we shall resist the temptation.
Heber J. Grant, CR 4/44:11

Resistance to temptation must come from within.
Richard R. Lyman, CR 10/35:22

Every temptation that comes to you and me comes in
one of three forms: (1) A temptation of the appetite or
passion; (2) A yielding to pride, fashion, or vanity; (3)
A desire for worldly riches or power and dominion
over lands or earthly possessions of men.
  David O. McKay, CR 10/63:8-9

When a man seeks something for nothing and shuns
effort, he is in no position to resist temptation.
  David O. McKay, CR 4/67:7

Your weakest point will be the point at which the
Devil tries to tempt you.
  David O. McKay, CR 10/59:88

The ones suffering the strongest temptations from evil
would likely be those living closest to evil.
  Sterling W. Sill, CR 10/62:38

Temptations without imply desires within.
  Sterling W. Sill, CR 4/70:29-30

The temptations up are far more pleasant and much
more profitable than the temptations down.
  Sterling W. Sill, CR 4/70:30

No temptation is a temptation, unless we are
entertaining it.
  Sterling W. Sill, CR 4/70:29

The man who is able to resist the temptation of those
things which appeal to his appetite, his physical
appetite, obtains power to overcome and resist evil in
all of its forms.
  Rulon S. Wells, CR 4/11:72

  See also: Forgiveness, Repentance, Satan, Sin

TESTIMONY

It is not necessary that one see an angel or hear a voice
from heaven in order to know that the gospel is true.
  Joseph Anderson, ACR 8/73:32

A testimony is not a destination; it is a possession for performance.
    Marvin J. Ashton, CR 4/72:61

A righteous man may die and pass from the earth, but his words of truth and testimony can not die and will not pass away, but they will live in the hearts of the people and bear fruit to the honor and the glory of God.
    Rudger Clawson, CR 4/19:39

There is no tangible, concrete evidence of the existence of God or the divinity of the Master in the legal sense, but not all inquiry for truth results in proof by real or demonstrative evidence.
    Howard W. Hunter, CR 4/75:57

Let us be pioneers (for our people yet to be born) by planting the wheat of our witness, that those who follow us may eat of the bread of belief in time of famine elsewhere in the world!
    Spencer W. Kimball, CR 4/76:70

The strength of the Church is not in the numbers, nor in the amount of tithes and offerings paid by faithful members, nor in the magnitude of chapels and temple buildings, but because in the hearts of faithful members of the Church is the conviction that this is indeed the church and kingdom of God on the earth.
    Harold B. Lee, CR 4/73:9

The most precious thing in the world is a testimony of the truth.
    David O. McKay, CR 10/64:92

Testimony and knowledge of God cannot be lost except through transgression.
    Henry D. Moyle, CR 4/63:46

Beware of the testimony of one who is intemperate, or irreverent, or immoral, who tears down and has nothing to put in its place.
    Boyd K. Packer, CR 4/74:138

252

The whole spirit world in the lower orders is full of deception, and unless you have something to detect and understand the true from the false you are liable to be led astray and destroyed.
Orson Pratt, JD 13:74

Men are not saved by virtue of their testimony alone.
Hartman Rector, Jr., CR 4/74:158

Testimonies can be acquired, testimonies can be kept, and testimonies can be lost.
Franklin D. Richards (1900, 1960-   ), CR 4/74:84

I would rather trust my boys and girls in this world with a testimony of this work burning in their souls than all the information you can give them out of all the schoolbooks that have ever been written.
LeGrand Richards, CR 10/46:124

This world is not big enough that you can run away from the testimony that the Lord plants in your heart.
LeGrand Richards, CR 10/51:167

I could live better without the limbs of my body than I could without the testimony of the Holy Ghost and the Spirit of the Lord.
LeGrand Richards, CR 4/52:112

Sin is disease and the testimony of Christ procures immunity from that disease.
Stephen L Richards, CR 10/25:118

No man had yet so much as heard of the Book of Mormon but what the Spirit of the Lord whispered quietly to his soul that that book was true: no man had so much as heard of the prophet Joseph Smith but what the "still small voice" whispered to him that he was a true prophet.
B. H. Roberts, CR 4/05:44

No matter how gifted we may be, or how choice our language, it is the spirit of our Father that reaches the heart and brings conviction of the divinity of this work.
George Albert Smith, CR 10/04:66

It is easier to talk about a testimony than to obtain one.
O. Leslie Stone, CR 4/75:10

✳ We gain testimony as we bear testimony.
A. Theodore Tuttle, CR 10/74:102

Argument has its mission, and God can inspire an argument just as readily as He can a testimony; but there is something peculiar about the power of testimony. It is a pioneer. Argument may come afterwards and fill up the gaps, build the bridges and the cities; but testimony goes before into the wilderness blazing a trail, and marking out the way.
Orson F. Whitney, CR 4/12:47

✓ Every human soul must push away the stone from the sepulchre, and know for himself that Christ is risen into life eternal.
Levi Edgar Young, CR 4/37:116

See also: Belief, Faith, Knowledge

THEFT

Men may succeed, by devious means, in taking property that does not belong to them, but such practices will destroy the moral fiber of their being.
Sylvester Q. Cannon, CR 10/34:87

Be very careful when you steal, for it is on interest from the time you steal it; for, remember, you do not get beyond the jurisdiction of the Almighty; and he will make you pay the uttermost farthing.
Ordon Hyde, JD 6:339

THEOCRACY

Priesthood is a perfect law of theocracy.
Joseph Smith, HC 5:555

THEOLOGY

Theology may be only diction, but religion requires action.
Hugh B. Brown, CR 10/62:41

Sectarian theology is the greatest tomfoolery in the world.
John Taylor, JD 5:240

THEORY

It is the specific performance of specific things that makes men better—not theory, not merely the fact that there is a set of principles or that there are commandments, or that there is counsel, but the living of it.
Richard L. Evans, CR 10/58:60

God does not deal in theories.
Richard L. Evans, CR 10/70:87

Do not forsake the wisdom of the ages for the theories of a Ph.D.
Stephen L Richards, CR 10/25:120

We have no right to take the theories of men, however scholarly, however learned and set them up as a standard, and try to make the Gospel bow down to them; making of them an iron bedstead upon which God's truth if not long enough, must be stretched out, or if too long, must be chopped off—anything to make it fit into the system of men's thoughts and theories! On the contrary, we should hold up the Gospel as the standard of truth, and measure thereby the theories and opinions of men.
Orson F. Whitney, CR 4/15:100

THOUGHTS

Those who think clean thoughts do not do dirty deeds.
Ezra Taft Benson, CR 10/64:60

Men and women think evil thoughts, they give place
to angry feelings; and they think it a meritorious act,
and pride themselves upon their conduct because they
give them utterance instead of quenching them. . . . It
is not hypocrisy to quench the evil thoughts that arise
in our minds.
George Q. Cannon, JD 21:78

A mind engrossed in sex is not good for much else.
J. Reuben Clark, Jr., CR 10/49:194

Any man who can't control his thoughts can't control
his actions, and any man who can't control his actions
isn't safe in society.
Richard L. Evans, CR 4/65:136

We may be faced with a lowered physical standard of
living, but we need not be faced with lowered
standards of thinking.
Richard L. Evans, CR 4/52:67

Just as rivers are colored by the substances picked up
as they flow along, so the streams of our thoughts are
colored by the material through which they are
channeled.
J. Thomas Fyans, CR 4/75:130

To develop good thoughts and acts, we must live and
associate with good people.
David B. Haight, CR 10/70:85

The key to every man is his thoughts.
Milton R. Hunter, CR 10/46:42

If one could look into your heart when you have
nothing in particular to do but to live with your
thoughts, one could predict your future happiness and
successes or your future heartaches and failures.
Milton R. Hunter, CR 4/63:15

Until we discipline our minds, and have the complete
control of them, we cannot make that advancement
that we ought.
Orson Hyde, JD 7:152

You are today where your thoughts have brought you.
You will be tomorrow, and the next day, and every
day where your thoughts will take you.
   Thorpe B. Isaacson, CR 10/56:12

It takes lots of courage to say always what you think.
The trouble is, we think things sometimes we ought
not to say.
   J. Golden Kimball, CR 4/10:53

We cannot think ugly thoughts or do ugly things
without retribution.
   Spencer W. Kimball, CR 4/74:128

There is no doubt that the life one leads and the
thoughts one thinks are registered plainly in his face.
   Spencer W. Kimball, CR 4/75:120

He approaches nearest the Christ spirit who makes
God the center of his thoughts.
   David O. McKay, CR 10/53:10

Thoughts that most frequently occupy the mind
determine a man's course of action.
   David O. McKay, CR 4/62:6

Upright character is the result only of continued effort
and right thinking, the effect of long-cherished
associations with Godlike thoughts.
   David O. McKay, CR 10/53:10

The strength of this Church lies in the purity of the
thoughts and lives of its workers.
   David O. McKay, CR 10/58:91-92

If we would change the world, we must first change
people's thoughts.
   David O. McKay, CR 10/64:5

The future safety of the world depends not so much
upon the changing of defenses as upon the changing
of men's way of thinking and acting.
   David O. McKay, CR 10/45:131

The brain, not the feelings or the passions, was designated by God to be the presiding officer of the personality.
 Sterling W. Sill, CR 10/63:78

One of our most urgent present-day needs is to houseclean our thinking.
 Sterling W. Sill, CR 10/59:103

The best way to improve our lives is to improve our thoughts.
 Sterling W. Sill, CR 10/59:103

Every thought tends to reproduce itself in an act.
 Sterling W. Sill, CR 4/55:118

The things of God are of deep import; and time, and experience, and careful and ponderous and solemn thoughts and reflections.
 Joseph Smith, HC 3:295

We become what we think about most.
 John H. Vandenberg, ACR 8/73:43

If you first gain power to check your words, you will then begin to have power to check your judgment, and at length actually gain power to check your thoughts and reflections.
 Brigham Young, JD 6:98

TIME

One of the most wasteful wastes in the world is the waste of time, of opportunity, of creative effort.
 Richard L. Evans, CR 10/70:87

Time is the essence of all our opportunities. It is the dimension in which we live. We can't speed it up, and we can't slow it down. We can't save it, and we can't hoard it. It is, in a sense, like manna from heaven.
 Richard L. Evans, CR 4/49:23

No man can limit the bounds or the eternal existence of eternal time.
Joseph Smith, HC 6:474

See also: Mortality

TITHING

No man can live the Order of Enoch who has not learned how to honestly live the law of tithing.
Melvin J. Ballard, CR 4/34:70

No man may hope or expect to have an inheritance on this celestial globe who has failed to pay his tithing.
Melvin J. Ballard, CR 10/29:51

The man who pays his honest tithing is paying his rent to the Almighty, who is the proprietor of this earth.
Melvin J. Ballard, CR 4/39:67

To me it is a marvel that any man having a testimony of the divinity of the work in which we are engaged as Latter-day Saints can sing lullabies to his conscience, figuratively speaking, and not be absolutely honest with the Lord in the payment of his tithes.
Heber J. Grant, CR 10/29:4

Some men get in debt and a few of them have told me that the Lord is so merciful and their creditors are so hard on them that they will pay them first.
J. Golden Kimball, CR 4/03:33

Tithing is not for God. It is we who clip the coupons and collect the dividends.
Spencer W. Kimball, CR 4/68:77

A person or a nation that will pay an honest tithing will never worship gold instead of God.
Thomas E. McKay, CR 4/46:151

The easiest and shortest way to get out of debt is to first pay our tithing, promptly and honestly.
Marriner W. Merrill, CR 4/03:66

We pay tithing with faith and not with money.
George Q. Morris, CR 4/53:111

If the entire membership of this Church paid their tithes honestly, there would never need to be another call on the people for anything in the building up of the kingdom of God.
Charles W. Nibley, CR 10/29:118

Tithing is an index of the faithfulness of the individual.
George F. Richards, CR 4/21:27

When we are through with this life and go hence, we will have no means with which to balance our tithing account.
George F. Richards, CR 4/48:19

I have found it to be a very difficult problem in mathematics to pay one-tenth out of one-twelfth.
Stephen L Richards, CR 4/29:53

If the Latter-day Saints do not obey the law that God has given with respect to the tithes, they will have less and less to tithe.
James E. Talmage, CR 10/30:74

How would you like the Lord to figure out his blessings on the same basis that you do when you are figuring out your tithing?
N. Eldon Tanner, CR 10/73:113

People do not pay tithing because they have money. They pay tithing because they have faith.
A. Theodore Tuttle, CR 4/70:86

The spiritual dividend that we draw from heaven as the reward of our obedience, is the principal purpose for which the Law of Tithing was instituted. All the rest is incidental or secondary.
Orson F. Whitney, CR 4/31:66

TONGUE

The tongue is merely the valve of the heart.
Orson Hyde, JD 6:151

If you want to know what hell fire is, just hear some
angry woman when she is rattling that little red rag—
the tongue.
Charles W. Penrose, CR 4/04:71

The tongue is the most dangerous, destructive and
deadly weapon available to man.
N. Eldon Tanner, CR 4/72:57

See also: Gossip

TRANSGRESSION

You never would complain of the sharpness of the
word of God, if you were not under transgression.
Heber C. Kimball, JD 5:173

Testimony and knowledge of God cannot be lost
except through transgression.
Henry D. Moyle, CR 4/63:46

I have found that it is very, very dangerous to fly just
high enough to miss the treetops.
Hartman Rector, Jr., CR 10/72:172

No one ever gets off the straight and narrow way at
right angles.
Sterling W. Sill, CR 4/65:88

Daily transgression and daily repentance is not that
which is pleasing in the sight of God.
Joseph Smith, HC 3:379

See also: Satan, Sin, Wrong

TRIALS

That which has sustained the Latter-day Saints

during their times of trial has been the spirit of prophecy.
  George Q. Cannon, CR 4/98:3

I believe that all Saints have their trials, if they are trying to do right and serve the Lord.
  Marriner W. Merrill, CR 10/97:4

From trial comes refined beauty.
  H. Burke Peterson, CR 10/73:12

From the depths of trial and despair have come some of the most beautiful and classic passages of modern-day scripture—not from the ease of a comfortable circumstance.
  H. Burke Peterson, CR 10/73:12

Trials are an evidence of a father's love.
  H. Burke Peterson, CR 10/73:12

A life filled with problems is no respector of age or station in life. A life filled with trials is no respector of position in the Church or social standing in the community.
  H. Burke Peterson, CR 10/73:11

God tries people according to the position they occupy.
  John Taylor, JD 24:197-98

Every trial and experience you have passed through is necessary for your salvation.
  Brigham Young, JD 8:150

TRUTH

No historic event is so important as the advent of a conviction of a new truth.
  Anon. Orson F. Whitney, CR 4/27:102

I am more interested in seeing the truth succeed than any organization to which I belong, but thank God, the organization to which I belong has the truth.
  Melvin J. Ballard, CR 4/32:61

Truth, if given as much time and emphasis as error, will invariably prove itself.
Ezra Taft Benson, CR 10/64:58

Truth is often on the scaffold—error on the throne. But time is on the side of truth, for truth is eternal.
Ezra Taft Benson, CR 10/64:58

Faith is not a substitute for truth, but a pathway to truth.
Hugh B. Brown, CR 10/69:107

Any open-minded search for truth requires courage, constancy, and humility.
Hugh B. Brown, CR 10/62:40

Every man that enters into this Church, if he understands the nature of his calling, understands that he enters into a warfare to contend for the triumph of truth.
George Q. Cannon, JD 25:254

If we value house, if we value lands, if we value good name, if we value even life itself more than we do the truth we are unworthy of the truth.
George Q. Cannon, JD 20:250

Searching for truth is an obligation. ✶
Richard L. Evans, ACR 8/71:173

A truth quietly spoken has much greater effect than an untruth shouted from the housetops.
Richard L. Evans, CR 10/38:91

A truth does not need to be shouted to be appreciated.
Richard L. Evans, CR 10/38:91

Truth has sprung from the earth, and righteousness has looked down from heaven, and they have met and have kissed each other.
Heber C. Kimball, JD 11:86

Truth is the sanctifier of those who love it and are guided by it, and will exalt them to the presence of God. ✶
Heber C. Kimball, JD 11:209

There is an eternal, undeviating principle that truth will prevail.
  Bruce R. McConkie, ACR 8/74:93

As the effulgent light of a glorious sun gladdens the surface of the earth by day, so the light of truth is entering into the hearts of many honest men and women throughout the world.
  David O. McKay, CR 4/62:8

Truth is loyalty to the right as we see it; it is courageous living of our lives in harmony with our ideals; it is always power.
  David O. McKay, CR 4/59:73

No man can be a true member of this Church and not love truth.
  David O. McKay, CR 4/68:7

If you have that testimony of truth on your side, you can pass through the dark valley of slander, misrepresentation, and abuse, undaunted as though you wore a magic suit of mail, that no bullet could enter, no arrow could pierce.
  David O. McKay, CR 4/58:130

Many elements of truth come only after a lifetime of preparation.
  Boyd K. Packer, CR 4/74:138

 Truth is not new; it may be revealed anew, and it may be new to the people to whom it is revealed. But there is only one plan of salvation, one true and everlasting gospel.
  Charles W. Penrose, JD 23:345

There are some truths greater than other truths.
  Franklin D. Richards (1821, 1849-1899), CR 10/98:31

Truth is a costly article, and always has been. It has cost the best men that have ever lived in the flesh, their mortal lives, and may yet again.
  Franklin D. Richards (1821, 1849-1899), CR 10/97:27

That which is good for man is true, and the gospel is good.
George F. Richards, CR 10/14:17

No man can hope to find out the truth without investigation.
George F. Richards, CR 4/12:41

A contrite heart is a fertile field for planting the seeds of truth.
Stephen L Richards, CR 4/39:41

Wherever we find truth, whether it exists in complete form or only in fragments, we recognize that truth as part of that sacred whole of which the Church of Jesus Christ is the custodian.
B. H. Roberts, CR 4/06:15

There can be no equal to the peace of mind that always comes as the reward for obedience to truth.
Robert L. Simpson, CR 10/67:19

We should gather all the good and true principles in the world and treasure them up, or we shall not come out true "Mormons."
Joseph Smith, HC 5:517

One truth revealed from heaven is worth all the sectarian notions in existence.
Joseph Smith, HC 6:252

Truth is "Mormonism."
Joseph Smith, HC 3:297

All I want is to get the simple, naked truth, and the whole truth.
Joseph Smith, HC 6:476

When things that are of the greatest importance are passed over by weak-minded men without even a thought, I want to see truth in all its bearings and hug it to my bosom.
Joseph Smith, HC 6:477

I have got all the truth which the Christian world possessed, and an independent revelation in the bargain, and God will bear me off triumphant.
  Joseph Smith, HC 6:479

There are none so blind as those who will not see, and none so deaf as those who will not hear; and there are none so heartless and so wicked as those who knowing the truth and seeing the light will close their eyes and their ears against it.
  Joseph F. Smith, CR 10/08:3

No people can ever prosper and flourish very long unless they can abide in God's truth.
  Joseph F. Smith, CR 4/05:5

The truth will never divide councils of the priesthood. It will never divide Presidents from their Counselors, nor Counselors from their Presidents, nor members of the Church from one another, nor from the Church.
  Joseph F. Smith, CR 4/07:4

When a man receives the truth he will be saved by it. He will not be saved merely because someone taught it to him, but because he received and acted upon it.
  Joseph F. Smith, CR 4/02:86

There is no science, nor philosophy that can supersede God Almighty's truth.
  Joseph F. Smith, CR 4/11:7

Truth does not grow old.
  Joseph Fielding Smith, CR 10/20:55

Truth always moves slowly.
  Reed Smoot, CR 4/02:25

The truth is frequently shocking just because of its simplicity and consequent grandeur.
  James E. Talmage, CR 4/15:121

A man in search of truth has no peculiar system to sustain, no peculiar dogma to defend or theory to uphold; he embraces all truth, and that truth, like the sun in the firmament, shines forth and spreads its effulgent rays over all creation, and if men will divest themselves of bias and prejudice, and prayerfully and conscientiously search after truth, they will find it wherever they turn their attention.

John Taylor, JD 16:370

Wherever we find truth, no matter where, or from what source it may come, it becomes part and parcel of our religious creed, if you please, or our political creed, or our moral creed, or our philosophy, as the case may be, or whatever you may please to term it.

John Taylor, JD 14:337

If there is any truth in heaven, earth, or hell, I want to embrace it, I care not what shape it comes in to me, who brings it, or who believes in it, whether it is popular or unpopular. Truth, eternal truth, I wish to float in and enjoy.

John Taylor, JD 1:155

We are open to truth of every kind, no matter whence it comes, where it originates, or who believes in it.

John Taylor, JD 16:369

People cannot change truth, but truth can change people.

John H. Vandenberg, CR 4/70:48

Truth has a native power of its own, and if stated clearly and fully it will be its own witness.

Orson F. Whitney, CR 4/30:46

Truth cannot contradict itself. If science and religion—true science and true religion—seem, in the least, to disagree, it is simply because man has not discovered enough, and God, perhaps, has not revealed enough, to bring us to the point of reconciliation; but that time will come.

Orson F. Whitney, CR 4/11:52-53

The test of truth is simplicity.

John A. Widtsoe, CR 4/21:37

With the sling of faith and the pebble of truth, like
David of old, we may lay low every giant of unbelief
and error and opposition to the truth in all the world.
  John A. Widtsoe, CR 4/45:93-94

Light is never found except in the presence of truth.
  John A. Widtsoe, CR 4/48:148

I suspect that one real difference between religion and
ethics is the manner in which truth is used.
  John A. Widtsoe, CR 10/21:47

No man can be a safe leader who does not love truth
above all else.
  John A. Widtsoe, CR 10/42:74

There is one thing in the world even greater than
truth, and that is the love of truth.
  John A. Widtsoe, CR 4/34:117

Truth is not an ornament to be hung on the wall or
placed on the shelf to look at. It must be of daily use.
  John A. Widtsoe, CR 4/47:75

It is easier to defend the truth than to defend error.
  Brigham Young, JD 19:42

The three great characteristics of creation are truth,
beauty, and goodness.
  Levi Edgar Young, CR 4/44:38

Truth has, it is quite true, but one enemy, and that is
untruth. Untruth has two enemies, truth and itself.
  Levi Edgar Young, CR 4/13:73

  See also: Falsehoods

UNITY

If you wait until everybody agrees in this Church, you
will be waiting through the second coming of the
Lord.
  Ezra Taft Benson, CR 4/65:124

An appreciation of diversification is the basis of unity.
Theodore M. Burton, CR 10/69:34

We shall never get to the place that the Lord expects us to go and marked out for us to get to, save we shall work together in unison.
J. Reuben Clark, Jr., CR 4/54:10

If there are to be distinctions among us, they must not be based upon our financial condition, but rather upon the principle of righteousness.
Rudger Clawson, CR 4/99:4

The key to a unified Church is a unified soul.
Howard W. Hunter, CR 4/76:157

Nothing can stay the progress of the kingdom of God as long as this mighty army of priesthood will keep united.
David O. McKay, CR 4/57:92

Unity is power.
Joseph Smith, HC 6:198

Without unity and confidence no faithful Latter-day Saint can be truly happy.
Joseph F. Smith, JD 25:51

VALUES

Times have changed only because people have changed them. But eternal values have not changed.
Thorpe B. Isaacson, CR 4/60:62

VIRTUE

Virtue lies at the foundation of greatness.
George Q. Cannon, JD 24:225

The home is the nursery not only of all human beings but of all virtue.
Stephen L Richards, CR 10/41:105

Virtue does not consist simply in being prevented
from committing evils, but in having temptations
presented before us and then governing our passions
and appetites.
John Taylor, JD 22:339

See also: Chastity, Morality

WAR

We are engaged in the greatest of all warfares.
George Q. Cannon, JD 11:229

I see a silver thread shining through the dark and
bloody tapestry of conflict.
Gordon B. Hinckley, CR 4/68:21

So fundamental in man's eternal progress is his
inherent right to choose, that the Lord would defend
it even at the price of war.
David O. McKay, CR 4/42:73

War is not the cause of the world's trouble; it is only
the outward manifestation of an inner decay.
Mark E. Petersen, CR 4/45:40

War doesn't solve a single human problem, and yet
the one place where our generation excels most is in its
ability to make war.
Sterling W. Sill, CR 4/66:21

It may be that the saints will have to beat their
ploughs into swords, for it will not do for men to sit
down patiently and see their children destroyed.
Joseph Smith, HC 6:365

WEAKNESS

Giving us weakness is one of the Lord's ways of getting
our attention.
Hartman Rector, Jr., CR 4/70:140

WEALTH

The man who seeks after the perishable things of this life and allows his mind to dwell upon them, to the exclusion of the things of God which pertain to his eternal salvation, has failed to comprehend the mission God has assigned him.
George Q. Cannon, JD 10:348

Anyone whose efforts are so set upon the things of this world, that he does not show fair dealings and mutual helpfulness to his fellowmen, though he may accumulate wealth, is a failure.
Sylvester Q. Cannon, CR 4/37:81

The riches of this earth are not the choicest the Lord has to bestow.
Matthias F. Cowley, CR 10/99:63

The tenderest part of a man's anatomy is his pocket.
Heber J. Grant, CR 4/12:29

Without labor there is neither wealth, nor comfort, nor progress.
Gordon B. Hinckley, CR 4/67:53

Purse-pride I think is meaner than any other pride.
Anthon H. Lund, CR 4/01:21

The rich can always take care of themselves—that is, so far as this world is concerned, I do not know how it will be about the next.
John Taylor, CR 4/80:62

The Lord does not care how wealthy a man becomes, so long as he holds his wealth for the building up of His kingdom, and for the carrying out of His purposes upon the earth.
Daniel H. Wells, JD 23:308

Pitiable is the poverty of the soul of one who works for earthly riches alone.
John Wells, CR 10/33:91-92

No man can rise very high who lives by earthly things
alone.
John A. Widtsoe, CR 4/40:38

As for riches and wealth, I do not want them if they
will damn me.
Wilford Woodruff, JD 18:39-40

To see the way that some people act, you might
suppose that they are going to live here eternally, and
that their eternal destiny depends upon the number of
dollars they have.
Wilford Woodruff, JD 18:120

Wealth never was the source of happiness to any
person. It cannot be: it is not in the nature of things;
for contentment exists only in the mind. In the mind
there is happiness—in the mind there is glory.
Brigham Young, JD 7:159

WELFARE

There is no need for any person in this Church to have
an empty mind, an empty hand, or an empty heart.
George Q. Morris, CR 4/52:31

No man has self-respect when he is the recipient of a
dole.
Marion G. Romney, CR 4/74:179

No true Latter-day Saint will, while physically able,
voluntarily shift from himself the burden of his own
support.
Marion G. Romney, CR 10/73:106

See also: Work

WISDOM

He who stops learning and working is neither wise nor
happy.
Charles A. Callis, CR 10/39:21

Wisdom is almost the greatest thing in the world, second only to health.
Heber J. Grant, CR 10/35:8

We cannot be turned from the wheat of the word of God, to the chaff that comes from the wisdom of man.
Joseph W. McMurrin, CR 4/06:27

To know what is best to say, what is best to do and know how best to do it is to possess inspired wisdom, probably our greatest gift.
Joseph F. Merrill, CR 10/40:77

An intellect governed by wisdom is man's proudest possession.
Joseph F. Merrill, CR 10/40:77

Perfect wisdom can come only from perfect knowledge.
B. H. Roberts, CR 10/25:147

There are a great many wise men and women too in our midst who are too wise to be taught; therefore they must die in their ignorance, and in the resurrection they will find their mistake.
Joseph Smith, HC 5:424

See also: Education, Knowledge

WOMANHOOD

If God made man "A little lower than the angels" (Ps. 8:5), he must then have made women his very angels.
William J. Critchlow, Jr., CR 10/65:39

A girl who sacrifices self-respect for social popularity debases true womanhood.
David O. McKay, CR 4/49:15

The test of true womanhood comes when woman stands innocent at the court of chastity.
David O. McKay, CR 4/49:15

The more woman becomes like man, the less he will
respect her; civilization weakens as man's estimate of
woman lessens.
  David O. McKay, CR 4/59:74

There is nothing in life so admirable as true manhood;
there is nothing so sacred as true womanhood.
  David O. McKay, CR 10/08:108

As females possess refined feelings and sensitiveness,
they are also subject to overmuch zeal, which must
ever prove dangerous, and cause them to be rigid in a
religious capacity.
  Joseph Smith, HC 5:19

No man, young or old, who holds the priesthood of
God can honor that priesthood without honoring and
respecting womanhood.
  N. Eldon Tanner, CR 4/73:124

Women are more ready to do and love the right than
men are.
  Brigham Young, JD 12:194

She who is worthy of the title of lady adorns her mind
with the rich things of the kingdom of God; she is
modest in her attire and manners; she is prudent,
discreet and faithful, and full of all goodness, charity,
love, and kindness, with the love of God in her heart.
  Brigham Young, JD 17:118

Ever since I knew that my mother was a woman I
have loved the sex, and delight in their chastity.
  Brigham Young, JD 12:194

  See also: Motherhood, Mothers

WORD OF WISDOM

The devil has never found a better tool in the history
of the world to destroy the happiness of human beings
than liquor.
  Milton R. Hunter, CR 10/66:40

The greatest menace or enemy which the Church of Christ has to combat is intemperance and sexual sin.
Anthony W. Ivins, CR 4/10:113

Were we more careful to obey the part of the word of wisdom that deals with the "do's" it might be easier to obey the "don'ts."
John A. Widtsoe, CR 4/26:110

See also: Body

WORK

Happy is the man who has work he loves to do. . . . Happy is the man who loves the work he has to do.
Anon. Adam S. Bennion, CR 4/55:111

Where nature does much for man, man is inclined to do little, or less; but where man has to struggle for his existence, there is the place where his physical powers are developed and his faith increased.
Melvin J. Ballard, CR 4/21:103

A good brain and the skill of man's right hand can produce wonders.
George Q. Cannon, JD 22:275

America stands in need of the gospel of strenuous work.
Charles A. Callis, CR 10/40:118

Work is the weapon of honor.
Charles A. Callis, CR 10/36:106

The greater the value of the object desired, the greater the effort required in its attainment.
Rudger Clawson, CR 10/14:78

Someone has to do everything that is done.
Richard L. Evans, CR 10/60:111

Work is a principle, a privilege, a blessing—not a curse—but an absolute essential, a physical and spiritual necessity.
Richard L. Evans, CR 10/70:87

✗ The aim of the Church is to help the people to help themselves. Work is to be re-enthroned as the ruling principle of the lives of our church membership.
  Heber J. Grant, CR 10/36:3

Without labor there is neither wealth, nor comfort, nor progress.
  Gordon B. Hinckley, CR 4/67:53

You are not living in the life of luck; it is a life of pluck, a life of effort and planning.
  Spencer W. Kimball, CR 4/75:117

✗ There is nothing more dangerous than idleness. . . . In labor there is salvation; in labor there is safety.
  Francis M. Lyman, CR 10/07:15

The old way of earning by our labor is the best way to become rich.
  Anthon H. Lund, CR 4/03:24

A skilled hand will always find work.
  Anthon H. Lund, CR 4/06:10

✗ There is no salvation without work.
  David O. McKay, CR 10/09:90

It is the things in life for which we are compelled to struggle that generally are worth the most to us.
  Henry D. Moyle, CR 4/58:65

All the fraudulent schemes, the rackets, governmental corruption, and wide-spread public demoralization have their inception and support chiefly in the failure to recognize the dignity and happiness that flow from honest toil.
  Stephen L Richards, CR 10/39:65

✗ The basis of God's perfect economic program is labor.
  Marion G. Romney, CR 10/73:105

One of the shortcomings of even the holy scriptures is that they are not automatic. That is, they will not work unless we do.
  Sterling W. Sill, CR 10/73:79

276

You can't do very well that which you don't enjoy doing.
Sterling W. Sill, CR 4/73:145

God has decreed that for everyone who falls in love with his work, his work shall live.
Sterling W. Sill, CR 10/75:43

The world owes me a living provided I will go to work to produce it by honest labor.
Joseph F. Smith, CR 4/98:49

It is not luck nor accident that helps a man in the world so much as purpose and persistent industry.
Reed Smoot, CR 4/34:37

Doing nothing is one of the hardest of all jobs. When you get tired, you can't rest. You are in bondage when you refuse to work.
Henry D. Taylor, CR 4/61:124

WORKING MOTHERS

Do without if you need to, but don't do without mother.
H. Burke Peterson, CR 4/74:44

Before you count the profit, count the cost of a working mother.
A. Theodore Tuttle, CR 4/67:94

See also: Motherhood

WORLD

Considering conditions in the world generally, there never was a time more cut off from Christ than ours, or one that needed him more.
Hugh B. Brown, CR 4/65:43

This world will be no better than its homes.
Richard L. Evans, ACR 8/71:71

Unless the world alters the course of its present trends
(and that is not likely); and if, on the other hand, we
continue to follow the teachings of the prophets, we
shall increasingly become a peculiar and distinctive
people of whom the world will take note.
    Gordon B. Hinckley, CR 10/74:143

We cannot survive spiritually with one foot in the
Church and the other foot in the world.
    Bruce R. McConkie, CR 10/74:44

Every world problem may be solved by obedience to
the principles of the gospel of Jesus Christ.
    David O. McKay, CR 4/20:116

You cannot pour the influences of the world into this
great solution of the gospel without diluting it.
    Stephen L Richards, CR 10/22:66-67

The world is making butterflies out of women and a
prison out of home.
    Stephen L Richards, CR 10/51:112

The whole world is fermenting with the leaven that
God planted when He brought this work into the
earth through the Prophet Joseph Smith.
    B. H. Roberts, CR 4/03:13

I do not expect enough people to repent to spare the
world from serious trouble.
    Marion G. Romney, CR 10/61:59

We are no better than the rest of the world, except to
the degree to which we accept the commandments of
the Lord and obey them.
    Marion G. Romney, CR 10/46:74

The world in which we live today is sick nigh to death.
The disease of which it suffers is not a new one. It is as
old as history. Its name is unrighteousness. The cure
for it is repentance.
    Marion G. Romney, CR 4/50:86

The world is not well. It is not dying yet, but it is sick.

It does not have an incurable disease, for we have a good physician.
Eldred G. Smith, CR 10/68:40

The world is full of technicalities and misrepresentation, which I calculate to overthrow, and speak of things as they actually exist.
Joseph Smith, HC 5:344

There is no cure for the ills of the world except the gospel of the Lord Jesus Christ.
Joseph Fielding Smith, CR 4/72:13

The only thing, it seems to me, that will save the world today is to acknowledge God and use good common sense.
Reed Smoot, CR 10/23:78

The future of the world depends on how we magnify the office which we hold in the priesthood.
N. Eldon Tanner, CR 10/75:112

When each man sets his own house in order, the whole world will be in order.
John A. Widtsoe, CR 10/36:98

Truth is my text, the Gospel of salvation my subject, and the world my circuit.
Brigham Young, JD 9:137

See also: Civilization, Society

WORSHIP

True and perfect worship consists in following in the steps of the Son of God.
Bruce R. McConkie, CR 10/71:168

True worship presupposes that men know whom they worship and know how to worship.
Bruce R. McConkie, CR 10/64:37

In our worship there are two elements: one is spiritual

communion arising from our own meditation; the other, instruction, from others, particularly from those who have authority to guide and instruct us. Of the two, the more profitable introspectively is meditation.
  David O. McKay, CR 4/67:85

There are two things I have always said I would do, and I calculate to carry them out, living or dying. One is to vote for whom I please and the other to worship God as I please.
  John Taylor, JD 14:338

If we turn from the Creator to the creature; if we forget the giver and adore the gift; if we forsake God and worship an emanation from God, we are idolaters, just as much as if we worshiped the sun and moon, or bowed down to goats and crocodiles.
  Orson F. Whitney, CR 4/20:121-22

If I were the emperor of the world and had control of every human being that breathes the breath of life on earth, I would give to every man, woman and child the right to worship God according to the dictates of their own conscience.
  Wilford Woodruff, JD 22:169

WRONG

Whatever is detrimental to health and happiness, or whatever impairs effectiveness or efficiency, is clearly wrong, morally wrong, spiritually wrong, as well as physically wrong.
  Richard L. Evans, CR 4/57:13

That which is wrong under one circumstance, may be, and often is, right under another.
  Joseph Smith, HC 5:135

Those who have done wrong always have that wrong gnawing them.
  Joseph Smith, HC 6:366

  See also: Transgression

If you want to keep young, go to where young people are; but if you want to get old, try to keep up with them.
Anon. Harold B. Lee, ACR 8/72:103

No one can begin to serve the Lord too early.
William H. Bennett, CR 4/75:86

✦ God reserved for these days some of his most valiant sons and daughters. He held back for our day proved and trusted children, who he knew from their premortal behavior would hear the voice of the shepherd and would accept the gospel of Jesus Christ.
Theodore M. Burton, CR 4/75:103

✦ God has reserved spirits for this dispensation who have the courage and determination to face the world, and all the powers of the evil one, visible and invisible, to proclaim the Gospel, and maintain the truth, and establish and build up the Zion of our God, fearless of all consequences.
George Q. Cannon, JD 11:230

Though the world is becoming more wicked, the youth of Christ's Church can become more righteous *if they understand who they are,* understand the blessings available, and understand the promises God has made to those who are righteous, who believe, who endure.
David B. Haight, CR 10/73:42

A happy home begins not at the marriage altar, but during the brilliant, fiery days of youth.
David O. McKay, CR 4/56:6

Youth without faith is a day without sun.
David O. McKay, CR 4/32:63

You might as well try to raise up an athlete on a diet of chocolate bars and soda pop as to attempt to sustain your youth with activity programs only.
Boyd K. Packer, CR 10/72:102

No effort to redeem your youth can be more productive than the time and attention given to priesthood home teaching.
Boyd K. Packer, CR 10/72:102

It seems to me that probably there has never been a time in the history of the world when there were as many of those spirits among whom the Father stood as there are upon the earth at the present time.
LeGrand Richards, CR 4/42:34

I believe this generation of young folk is the finest and the cleanest, the most intelligent, and the best educated group we have had for as long as I know anything about the missionary service.
S. Dilworth Young, CR 4/49:95

When the Lord God has wanted to train great leaders for his eternal purposes, he has not hesitated to choose boys, call them, anoint them, prepare them, and then when grown send them forth to their allotted destiny.
S. Dilworth Young, CR 10/74:130

See also: Children, Family

ZION

We ought to have the building up of Zion as our greatest object.
Joseph Smith, HC 3:390

The whole of America is Zion itself from north to south.
Joseph Smith, HC 6:318-19

God is at the helm of the ship Zion, and He will never allow it to run upon the rocks.
Reed Smoot, CR 4/07:31

We shall not have 365 years as Enoch had to prepare Zion for translation.
Wilford Woodruff, JD 12:280

See also: Church, Latter Days, Mormonism